FREE RADICAL

FREE
RADICAL

New Century Essays

TONY BENN

continuum

NEW YORK • LONDON

Continuum

The Tower Building
11 York Road
London SE1 7NX

15 East 26th Street
New York
NY 10010

www.continuumbooks.com

© Tony Benn 2003

These articles were originally published by the *Morning Star* 2001–2002
This collection first published by Continuum 2003

This edition published 2004

British Library Cataloguing-in-Publication Data
A catalogue record for this book is available from the British Library.

ISBN 0–8264–7400–4

Typeset by RefineCatch Limited, Bungay, Suffolk
Printed and bound by MPG Books Ltd, Bodmin, Cornwall

Contents

List of Abbreviations

AEA	Atomic Energy Authority
AFL–CIO	American Federation of Labor–Congress of Industrial Organizations
ANC	African National Congress
ASLEF	Associated Society of Locomotive Engineers and Firemen
BNP	British National Party
CIA	Central Intelligence Agency
CND	Campaign for Nuclear Disarmament
CWU	Communications Workers' Union
EU	European Union
FBU	Fire Brigades Union
GMB	General, Municipal and Boilermakers' union
ILO	International Labour Organization
IMF	International Monetary Fund
LEA	Local Education Authority
NATO	North Atlantic Treaty Organization
NPT	Non Proliferation Treaty
NUJ	National Union of Journalists
NUM	National Union of Mineworkers
OFSTED	Office for Standards in Education
PCS	Public and Commercial Services union
RMT	Rail, Maritime and Transport Union
TGWU	Transport and General Workers' Union
TUC	Trades Union Congress
UPW	Union of Post Office Workers
WTO	World Trade Organization

Foreword

The *Morning Star* is a newspaper that every member of the Labour movement should read because it gives news and information from all over the world about the struggles of working people – for peace, democracy and human rights – that are not normally published in the British press.

Looking back over the years, from the time that it was known as the *Daily Worker*, this paper has taken a strongly anti-fascist, anti-racist, anti-imperialist line, and with the end of Stalinism it has been freed from some of the pressures that were placed on it as a result of its uncritical loyalty to the Soviet Union.

Its contributors include communists and socialists and trade unionists, whose opinions, once marginalized, now have a resonance with many people who have come round from the ideological domination of the Thatcher era, and the seductive simplicities of New Labour, to see the need for progressive change.

I was therefore very honoured to be asked to write for the *Morning Star* when I left parliament. I have found the challenge a difficult one, but it has given me the opportunity to try to clarify my thinking on the issues which face this country.

Since September 11 the world has changed fundamentally, and at the time of writing it appears that President Bush is determined to wage war on Iraq and the Prime Minister is determined to support him even if no United Nations mandate is given. This is a very dangerous policy and as we confront American imperialism we can see many of the gains made years ago being threatened and the UN itself being undermined.

At home the New Labour Government appears ready to break with the trade unions. It has long ago abandoned any serious socialist commitment, so that the philosophy of monetarism seems to be entrenched in its thinking. It is also a very centralizing government, leaving us with a president but no House of Representatives, little Cabinet authority and no effective link with the Labour Party nationally through its annual conference.

The growth of the multinational companies, the media moguls, the World Trade Organization (WTO), the International Monetary Fund (IMF), and the European Union (EU) under the authority of the Commission and the Frankfurt bankers, all threaten our democratic rights and could return us to a state of disenfranchisement from which we began to emerge in the nineteenth century.

I hope that readers of these articles will be encouraged to subscribe to the *Morning Star* and contribute their news and views to strengthen it in the years that lie ahead, when its role will become even more important.

Looking ahead, it has become increasingly clear to me that if we are to make any progress at all we have to do it through our own organizations, seeking to explain the real world and mobilize people to put pressure on the government that it simply cannot disregard.

My reading of history is that this is how all progress has been made, whether we are looking at the end of slavery, the birth of trade unionism, the extension of the franchise to men and women, the ending of apartheid or the growth of the environmental movement.

All these movements are in being and millions of people all over the world are engaged in trying to advance these causes and uniting against globalization and war, and arguing for policies that would produce justice. We can see it in America too, where a very strong peace movement is upholding all that is best in the American political tradition, against a president who is trying to dominate, as all imperial leaders do.

We see it in Europe and in Latin America; and with the development of the Internet it has been possible to organize conferences that bring people together and develop programmes that, even if the media ignore them, are winning wider and wider public support.

Clearly the dangers of modern warfare with chemical, biological and nuclear weapons could threaten the survival of the human race in a way that no previous wars have ever done. But the technology at our disposal now, if properly redirected, offers prospects of improvement on a scale that even the most visionary people never could have imagined.

Therefore the choices we face are moral, practical and political questions, requiring international cooperation and democracy operating across frontiers to revitalize the UN as the only effective challenge to imperial power.

For this reason it is a thrilling period in which to live. The *Morning Star* challenges the existing orthodoxy, warns us of the dangers and points the way forward to an audience that goes well beyond the ideological Left, appealing to all progressive people who share these aspirations.

Tony Benn, December 2002

1

Old Labour

Turning the tide

For years the Left has been on the defensive against policies which it believed damaged the interests of those the Labour movement was created to defend. There was a major campaign at the end of the 1970s when the IMF imposed severe cuts on public expenditure that opened up the way for the Tories to return to power. During the Thatcher years, we were engaged in campaigns to protect the trade unions and local government, and later against the Gulf War. Margaret Thatcher argued that there was no alternative, and this demoralized a lot of people who were actually persuaded that even if they made the effort it would be bound to fail, so they contracted out of politics altogether.

In those long opposition years we were told that if Labour were to have any chance of getting back to power it would have ditch its core beliefs and come to terms with capitalism. Since 1997, after New Labour came to power, the Left has worked to stop the leadership from abandoning its commitment to socialism and the Labour movement, and from seeking to link up with the Liberals and some 'wet' Conservatives to form a centre party around the Third Way. Throughout this period we have been either vilified by the media or marginalized as 'Old Labour' whose opinions could be safely dismissed as having no relevance and no public support.

Some good socialists became disillusioned and opted out of the work of the party; others actually left, while a few have decided to work for the creation of a new social-ist alliance that intends to put up candidates against us in the election. Those who now argue along these lines have said that the Labour Party is dead and that our only hope lies in replacing it as the Labour Party replaced the Liberal Party years ago.

Of course many of the criticisms we hear are echoed inside the party, but far from being tempted to throw in the towel my own regret is that so many good comrades should have left us when their membership alongside us would have strengthened the Left in the Labour Party. Anyone of course can put up for parliament, and those who are planning to stand as candidates are quite entitled to do so, but it will weaken Labour in some constituen-cies, and by splitting the vote could actually help Liberals and Tories to win there. In industrial struggles we are often reminded that 'Unity is strength', and I believe that this is true in political struggles too.

But perhaps the most powerful argument for unity is that the tide is now turning and we have no reason to see ourselves as lone campaigners fighting against the odds or voices in the wilderness. Public opinion is actually moving towards an acceptance of what the Left has been saying, as we have seen with the overwhelming support for the renationalization of the railways and opposition to privatization of Air Traffic Control, the London Underground and the private finance initiatives in health and education.

There are now people across the whole political spectrum who see the dangers posed by the American national missile defence system and who have also begun to appreciate the dangers posed by having our economy controlled by European bankers and commissioners who we do not elect and cannot remove. There are also many young people, both in this country and world-wide, who realize that globalization poses a direct threat to democracy.

The Left should therefore now be looking ahead and campaigning, during the election and after, for the policies we want to see implemented, and widening its appeal well beyond the party. I believe that this is exactly what will happen, provided the policies we put forward are positive, as is the case with the peace movement and the pensioners, where what is being said is common sense and is accepted as such.

For years it has been the deliberate policy of many political leaders to lower public expectations. Those tactics have been successful in spreading defeatism and gloom which has reduced the pressure for social justice from underneath. Half the time we are told we have a most successful economy and the other half we are warned that we cannot afford the policies that we really need. All this needs to be challenged, and that challenge is essential when Labour begins its second term in office this summer. Certainly no socialist needs to shy away from saying what he really believes, because there is now a large audience outside waiting to hear it.

16 March 2001

A Tribute to British Communists

On Wednesday, in Chesterfield, there was a crowded memorial meeting for Fred Westacott who, well into his eighties, died recently after a lifetime of dedicated service to socialism.

Fred was a life-long Communist, once a full-time organizer for the party, and an inspiration to everyone who knew him, and certainly to me since I first came to the town nearly twenty years ago. His death, and the response it has evoked, encourages me to pay a tribute not only to him, but to all those who have worked in the Communist Party over the years, and who have made a tremendous contribution to the trade union, Labour and peace movements and to the pensioners' movement, to which Fred devoted himself in recent years.

It is time this was recognized and recorded, since communists have been denounced and reviled by the British establishment, and by most Labour Party leaders, since the Russian Revolution which they supported. And during the Cold War here, and the witch-hunt launched by Senator McCarthy against the Left in America, all members of the Communist Party were systematically blacklisted by every employer and kept under automatic surveillance by the security services as potential traitors and subversives. One unexpected side-effect of this was to frighten off, or weed out, from the party anyone whose main ambition was to get on in politics, or the trade union movement, leaving only the most dedicated to carry on for no reason other than their commitment to the cause.

Yet despite all these difficulties the Communist Party, banned as it was from affiliation to the Labour Party, remained a university of socialism, working in the trade unions and thus influencing the thinking of the unions that *were* affiliated to Labour and keeping Marxist ideas on the political agenda. Moreover, during the 1930s it was the Communist Party that played a leading role in fighting fascism, supporting the Spanish workers in their war against the Franco dictatorship and in the unemployed workers' movement in Britain.

The main charge levelled against the Communist Party – that it was just the unthinking agent of the Kremlin – was based upon a misunderstanding of their view that world-wide support was necessary if the Soviet Union was to survive the attacks from its many enemies.

(And how true was the immense courage of the Russian people who bore the brunt of the German armies and gave us the breathing space we needed to win the war!)

It is true that the British party made a mistake in 1939 when it opposed the British declaration of war against Germany and only changed its policy when Hitler invaded Russia in 1941. But the charge that it uncritically sup-ported all the excesses during the Stalinist period conveniently ignores the fact that those excesses were not widely known, even in the Soviet Union, until Khruschev's famous speech which disclosed them.

Less intelligible to many was the passionate ideological hatred by the Communist Party of anyone and everyone who had a good word to say about Trotsky, who is entitled to his place in history and indeed has inspired some of the younger activists on the Left today.

The greatest damage done to the party came from inside, with the emergence of the postmodernists (expressed through the pages of *Marxism Today*) which began to erode both its unity and influence. Indeed, some of the revisionists found themselves attracted by the democratic centralism preached by the commissars in the Millbank Tower.

But happily the likes of Fred Westacott, and many others in the Communist Party, kept the faith and made a tremendous contribution to the Left. This has been at a time when more and more people seek a better explanation of what has gone wrong than the conventional wisdom which lays all the blame on those who have not modernized their thinking to get us to love global capitalism and surrender our democratic rights to the Brussels Commission, the Central Bank, the WTO and the IMF.

When I look back at those who have worked hardest for peace and pensions, for trade union rights and full employment, and for democracy, many of them were communists. As a lifelong Labour Party member, I would have preferred to have had them inside the Labour Party. However, they were not allowed in and were not prepared to make the sacrifice of principle that would have been involved in giving up their faith to join us.

Looking ahead to the next decade, it is certain that the broad Left will need to think of ways to make its influence felt more strongly, and that must mean winning the Labour movement to socialism, again, as Keir Hardie did a hundred years ago.

And in making this possible we shall need more communists like Fred Westacott.

12 April 2001

Democracy must be our theme

After the election, the Labour and socialist movement has got to be positive and forward-looking if it is to win support for the work it has to do. With Labour back in office, we shall be reminded that lay-offs and redundancies have to be accepted as market decisions in a global economy and that our economic policy must be controlled by the EU and the IMF. Privatization will be extended into health and education on a big scale, and we shall be told that welfare reform means shifting from benefits as of right to a means-tested system.

These policies would effectively involve dismantling the Labour Party as we know it and embracing capitalism and capitalist values, softened only by a few charitable concessions to the poor. To meet this challenge socialists should be pushing the frontiers of democracy much further forward and making demands upon the government which would extend popular control in areas where it has never really existed.

The nationalized industries increased investment, improved working conditions and recognized trade union rights, but they never got near the point of being democratic since workers had no role in the administration of these industries. Compare that to the demands made in 1919 by Thomas Straker, Secretary of the Northumberland Miners' Association, who argued that every miner: 'must have a share in the management of the industry in which he is engaged and . . . must feel that the industry is being run by him in order to produce coal for the use of the community instead of profit for the few'.

We should renew that demand for industrial

democracy and include it in the workers' rights which must be established and embodied in law. This is the best way to make the power of international corporations accountable, not only to their shareholders but to those who create the wealth which they own. If that were done we might be able to limit the crude abuse of business power which we have seen recently, for instance, by Corus, Ford, General Motors and Motorola.

Public ownership must be extended and strike action must be entrenched as a right, but even in the public services there is very little industrial democracy and those who do withdraw their labour to protect the public interest can alienate the very people they are trying to help. For example if the RMT and ASLEF were to campaign on the trains with leaflets about safety and public ownership they might find it as effective as a stoppage, and it would be much harder for those who did it to be taken to the courts and issued with an injunction.

Similarly in hospitals, where doctors, nurses and other staff have a strong sense of vocation, they might consider taking control of the hospitals from the managers as a form of industrial action and making it their business to see that every patient and visitor knew exactly why they were doing so and why their arguments matter to the community at large. This technique might also be used in schools, since strikes by teachers can cause anxieties amongst parents whose children have examinations to take, and there is a case for ring-fencing such examination students and teaching them intensively during industrial action, whilst opening the rest of the school to be a centre where everyone in the area could bring their own problems, discuss them and get support for their own campaigns. In this way the unions would be seen to be on the side of people, defending democratic rights, and there is a good chance that this would have an appeal well beyond the ranks of the movement and so become a majority view.

Democracy too should be the centrepiece of our arguments on Europe, where we should argue actively for European cooperation but insist that every law and move towards harmonization must be explicitly approved by the elected parliaments of each member-state and not imposed on any nation.

We should also demand that all the members of the UN General Assembly should be elected in each country, just as we elect members of the European parliament, and that that UN General Assembly should elect the Security Council which would have power to control the WTO, the IMF and the multinational corporations.

In setting out this vision of a democratic future we should be doing no more than the Chartists did 150 years ago, or the African National Congress when it called for an end to white rule.

If as socialists we make democracy and internationalism our central theme we can put the advocates of global capitalism on the defensive, including some who may hold high office in the incoming New Labour government.

29 May 2001

Rebuilding the movement

The election is over and it looks like a big Labour majority for a second term on a manifesto that is probably the most conservative ever put before the electorate by the Labour Party. Having campaigned in 25 constituencies for a Labour victory, which I desperately wanted to see take place, much work now has to be done if we are going to rebuild the Labour movement to achieve its historic task of representing working people and seeing that their interests are safeguarded.

We shall, no doubt, be told that there is a massive mandate for the privatization of the public services – including health, education and the Post Office – and the pensioners must abandon their demand for a link with earnings and be satisfied with a means-tested system. The rich, who were afraid they might be asked to pay more income tax at the higher levels, have been reassured, and the British establishment has got what it wanted – a government committed to globalization able to rely on the Labour movement to support it in carrying through all these policies.

If this programme is allowed to go through parliament, and Britain is to be brainwashed into believing that the Central Bank in Frankfurt should be trusted with the control of our economy, the Commission to make our laws and the multinationals to control our industry, we shall in effect have wound up any semblance of democratic control of our future. The only way that this can be prevented is by rebuilding the Labour movement from the bottom up and seeking to win it back for socialist ideas and values so as to provide a genuine alternative to the government's agenda. This means that the trade unions have to campaign vigorously for the repeal of the anti-trade union laws and against the privatization which would destroy the public services.

If we are to do this, the Labour conference will be absolutely crucial, and trade union delegates and members of the National Executive Committee and National Policy Forum have got to be absolutely clear about what they will and will not accept, and use their power and the Brighton conference to change the direction of party policy to meet these requirements.

It must mean that Labour councillors come out strongly for a revitalized local democracy where elected councillors wrest back the powers of initiative from Whitehall, and the quangos and tsars and managers who are trying to take over their function and turn them into agents of the presidential system which we now seem to accept. We shall also need MPs who have got the guts to hold the government to account by wresting from the Whips' office the power they now have to control the committee members and insisting that the laws made in Brussels are subjected to a parliamentary vote before British ministers are allowed to agree to them in Brussels. All patronage must be subjected to the approval of the House of Commons in the way the Senate has to approve presidential appointments in the United States. The House of Lords must be replaced by a fully elected chamber, free of the crony system which has crept in as part of a so-called reform.

If any of these things are to be achieved, the Left in Britain has got to rally itself together and work harmoniously, abandoning its sectarian habits which are so deeply engrained.

I can well understand why socialist candidates wanted to put up in the election, but our problem in Britain is that we have too many socialist parties and not enough

11

socialists. The basis of our unity must now be around the issues that need to be tackled and not as part of a futile attempt to find a common ideology as if we were religious sects and not practical men and women. The danger we face if we do not achieve this is the complete Americanization of British politics, where big business buys both major political parties and expects a pay-off whichever one wins. If this comes to pass it would mean the complete marginalization of all popular movements.

For the first time in my life, the public are to the left of the Labour Party, and so we must not assume that in calling for all this we are separating ourselves from the main body of opinion. But we do have to persuade them by argument and good organization, and offer some sort of an explanation of what is happening in place of the shallow, personalized and abusive nature of the recent election campaign.

We have this advantage over the pioneers who founded the movement in the nineteenth century, when the Tolpuddle Martyrs and the Chartists began their work, for they simply didn't have any reason to believe they could achieve anything. We, by contrast, have 150 years of experience in trying to build a better world, and we have had some successes and some failures, and we have to learn from them.

For all these reasons, this is no time for socialists to be depressed, for what has to be done has to be done, and it will only be done by working together, here and world-wide, with determination, persistence and hope.

8 June 2001

Unity is strength

The decision of the some trade unions to cut back their financial support for the Labour Party and spend the money on campaigning on the issues which most concern their own members is entirely understandable, since they are faced with mass privatization imposed by a government which has refused to repeal the anti-labour legislation enacted by the Tories and has not even agreed to bring our laws into line with the ILO convention to which Britain is a signatory. But it would be an absolute disaster if any union affiliated to the party were to sever the link or even reduce their affiliation fees in such a way as to diminish the votes which they have at the Labour conference, for not only would that delight New Labour, who greatly dislike the union connection, but it would gravely damage the prospects of Labour ever being rescued from New Labour which is rapidly losing its support within the party as a whole.

What has distinguished the British Labour Party from other social democratic parties world-wide has been that organic link with the trade unions who set the party up and have often saved it from those on the Right who, in the past, tried to destroy it.

It must be obvious to any progressive person that those who are hoping for a government that actually adopts progressive policies and is able to win an election to implement them must first be able to win over the Labour Party and move from there to a wider national campaign. Those who blame Labour as a whole for what New Labour is doing and desert the party, are bound to damage their own cause.

I can understand those who, out of disappointment or disgust, leave the Labour Party but this is bound to weaken the prospects for achieving what they have in mind, which must, inevitably, require the backing of the trade unions and the Labour Party if it is to succeed.

The Communist Party carries on a fine tradition that has helped to educate thousands of people in an understanding of socialism. Arthur Scargill, one of the greatest living trade union leaders, whose work for the miners will never be forgotten, has set up his own party, the Socialist Labour Party, but puts up candidates against the Socialist Alliance, led by Liz Davies, whom I know and greatly admire. This party, by contrast, works with the Socialist Party, which includes brilliant men such as Dave Nellist, and they can work with the Socialist Workers' Party, which has played a leading role in the anti-globalization and Stop the War campaigns, while in Scotland the Scottish Socialist Party led by Tommy Sheridan – a very fine socialist – works with passion and integrity for progressive policies. These people are all dedicated, as was the Independent Labour Party, which disaffiliated from Labour when Ramsay MacDonald was prime minister but, having left us, withered away as a serious force. I suspect that the same could happen to those who today have followed the same course, for unity is strength in political as well as industrial struggles.

Of course it is argued that one, or more, of these socialist groupings might actually replace the Labour Party in the way that the fledgling Labour Party replaced the Liberal Party in the 1920s, but even if that did happen (which I doubt), it might take half a century, and the result could only be the creation of a new sort of party that was wide and broad in its political composition – rather like the Labour Party is today.

Such a project would have to overcome another difficulty if it were to succeed, namely the fact that socialist campaigning has to be based upon the representation of working-class interests and cannot survive on ideological lectures that tend to be so strict in their interpretation of their faith that the result is divisive rather than unifying. We saw this in France when three Left candidates actually fought each other and helped to pave the way for Le Pen's success in the first round of the French parliamentary elections.

Anger and frustration at New Labour also takes the form of denunciations of those New Labour leaders who are held to have betrayed the movement and, though the charge of personal betrayal may help to inject passion into a controversy, those who face real problems such as unemployment, homelessness, poverty or discrimination necessarily want to see their difficulties addressed directly; they are not interested in those who seem to be primarily concerned with denouncing others.

What we have to do is to redirect all our efforts towards achieving a majority for the policies we need, and our socialist analysis helps us to understand the situation but our theoretical differences must not be allowed to divide us, and there is no reason whatever why we should not all be able to speak with anyone else on platforms that express our common purpose.

When it comes to polling day, everyone has to make up his or her mind as to which candidate they wish to vote for, but elections come only every five years and polling day is, therefore, only one of 1812 days in that period,

15

so that it is what we do between elections that matters most.

I am a Labour man. I joined on my birthday, 60 years ago, and intend to die in the party. What keeps me going is the trade union link, the good socialists still in the party, and what Labour could become if we work together in a spirit of goodwill, and above all share the belief that it can be done, because our own history should tell us that the pioneers overcame obstacles greater even than we face.

5 July 2002

After New Labour

Those on the Left who passionately believe that the Labour Party is dead and cannot recover, including those who resigned because they had become disillusioned, would do well to study what is actually going on in the party.

Last Saturday in Durham thousands marched proudly through the streets of the city with bands and banners representing many different trade unions from across the country, as well as those from the pits which have been closed, and the spirit was uplifting. Later, on the race-course, where the Big Meeting (as it is called) was held, the speakers, including Veronica Dunn, president of Unison, John Edmonds from the GMB and Jeremy Corbyn, all argued for the public services, against pri-vatization, for a fair tax system, better pensions, the restoration of trade union rights and a return to inter-nationalism against those who present globalization as the answer to all the world's problems. The response from the huge crowd which had gathered there – the biggest for years – was unmistakeable, and no one who was present could doubt for a moment that this was a gathering of loyal Labour supporters who had come to give their backing to those arguing for real social progress.

Tomorrow, at the TUC headquarters in Congress House in London, the campaign group is holding its third socialist conference called 'After New Labour' which will be looking to the future and arguing for positive policy initiatives that we should be supporting once the spin-doctors and focus groups which have been peddling Third Way illusions, as a part of the ill-fated project cooked up to replace the Labour Party with some centre coalition, come to be rejected – as they will be. The papers that have been prepared – and which I hope will be widely publicized and read within the movement – cover the future of the welfare state, race and nationality, economic policy, democracy, the future of the public services, justice and the legal system, sustainability and the international situation, including one by Noam Chomsky.

All this is taking place against the background of a looming world economic crisis, made worse by corruption and deceit in some major world corporations, which has shaken confidence and threatens millions whose pensions may be at risk at a time when the state pensions are being allowed to decline in relation to earnings.

The substantial increases in public spending announced by the Chancellor on Monday, which are long overdue, may help to counteract the downturn, and President Bush is banking on his massive boost to US military expenditure to put some money into the American economy (a technique used by the interwar dictators to get Germany and Italy out of the slump then). But none of these moves will deal with the growing insecurity felt by so many millions who fear for their jobs as market forces tighten their grip and in their desperate search for higher profits ruthlessly lay off workers or move the work overseas where wages are lower.

Even those employed in the public services here have been warned that, if they do not agree to what is called modernization, the pace of privatization may be stepped up; and war preparations, which may create jobs in the arms industry, also create a sense of anxiety in the public as a whole that more wars are being planned which no one wants. Insecurity can be very dangerous politically because frightened people may be tempted to follow some demagogue who looks for scapegoats and builds his or her power-base on stimulating fear. For this reason socialists who are serious must make their message reassuring and positive.

Our proposals must also be practical, and be seen to be so, if we want the public to support us as some of the extreme language that is used on the Left actually frightens people who would otherwise want to back us. Clem Attlee was known for speaking of 'workmanlike plans' to justify revolutionary proposals such as the creation of the welfare state and the NHS, whereas if he had shouted his head off about the need to 'smash the state' it might have put people off.

For these reasons I suspect that some of the arguments between reform and revolution may be a bit misleading, since genuine revolutionaries would be secretly undertaking military training to prepare themselves to storm Buckingham Palace, as if this was St Petersburg in 1917; when actually a society that peacefully opted for policies that put need before profit, and won a majority for this, would be infinitely more revolutionary in its impact. If we want to win that majority for change we have to address people's real problems, work out how to solve them and not lecture them about our ideology as if we were academics teaching a course in Marxism, though without a socialist analysis it is impossible to understand what is going on, why and work out how we can best deal with it.

Socialism also allows us to understand our own history better and to know what works best. It should provide the moral basis for what we say and do, which is essential if we are to take the right decisions about our future and help people to organize themselves through the trade union movement and other progressive organizations, nationally and internationally, which is what we have to do and why democracy is so important.

What we need now is more confidence in ourselves.

20 July 2002

2

New Labour

The myth of modernization

The word 'modernization' is being used by New Labour to justify all the most old-fashioned policies that it is introducing, and it is time we looked at what it really means.

Take, for instance, the so-called modernization of the public services, which involves the handing over of schools and hospitals to private companies to build and manage. That was the way it was all done a hundred years ago, before the welfare state was created, when those who could afford to pay got the services they needed, while the rest were lucky if they received a bit of charity. New Labour wants to go back to that – and calls it modernization.

Or take the minimum guarantee for pensioners to replace the state pension linked to earnings, introduced by the Labour government. This takes us right back to the hated means test which we rejected in 1945 – and they call it modernization.

It is the same with our educational system, where we are being told that to modernize our schools we have to go back to selection, as happened with the eleven-plus that kept the grammar schools for the so-called gifted children and shunted the rest onto the labour market, trained to obey but not to think. Chris Woodhead gave the impression that he hated the idea of educating working-class children, but of course it was all dressed up as modernizing to improve standards.

Or take imperialism under Queen Victoria, when Britain ruled the world and had troops in Africa and Asia holding down the local populations so that we could get cheap raw materials and find an easy market for our goods to make a profit. Now Britain slavishly follows America, with its plan to dominate the world through its military bases all designed to safeguard the interests of the United States and its need for oil and markets – and we are told we have to modernize.

And what about Star Wars, which will trigger a new arms race which did so much damage to our economy during the Cold War? That is being justified to modernize our defences.

It is the same with the so-called modernization of the House of Lords, now being stuffed with the Prime Minister's cronies, just as the king did hundreds of years ago before we won the vote and were able to elect and remove those who made the laws we were expected to obey. The House of Commons itself is being treated with the same contempt, as the Prime Minister sacks Gwyneth Dunwoody and Donald Anderson who, as chairs of important select committees, dared to criticize his policies.

The modernization of parliament means that MPs are treated like puppets on a string all controlled by Downing Street. And we now have 'tsars' to take over important projects, instead of leaving it to elected local authorities who are close to the people and represent them rather than manage them. It makes you wonder whether New Labour are not living in the Winter Palace in St Petersburg and regard the populace as the mob who must be kept at bay.

New Labour has brainwashed and bullied the Labour movement into giving up the internal democracy we won to allow constituencies and affiliated unions to push resolutions right up to the annual conference and get them into our manifesto. All that has been dismantled, and a mass of policy forums with no real power have been set up to filter out the policies that are not acceptable to the Millbank Tower – a system they also describe as modernization.

The main responsibility for all this rests with the leadership, but those who go along with it, who keep their heads down and mutter privately but do nothing, are equally responsible because it is their silence that makes all this possible.

Sometimes when I make this point, party members will agree but say that they do not know what to do to change it – as if they feel themselves to be absolutely powerless in the face of a juggernaut that cannot be stopped. But it is not as difficult as it may seem, for all we have to do is to speak our minds openly and without personal abuse, and vote for what we believe in, wherever we are, and organize and persuade others to do the same.

Above all we must expose, ridicule and oppose all those who try to sell us right-wing, old-fashioned, outdated ideas as if they were the latest example of modernization. For the plain truth is that New Labour is regurgitating some of the very worst practices from the past and trying to pass them off as brand-new.

We must look ahead and, if we do, we can see what needs to be done, which is to build a society based upon morality and social justice, peace and internationalism, democracy and human rights – and if we succeed we would then be well ahead of our time and would be seen as the real modernizers.

20 July 2001

New Labour bans conscience

The interview between Paul Marsden and the Chief Whip, as reported in the press, has thrown an entirely new light on the real meaning of New Labour, for, if the account given by Paul is correct, he was told that Labour MPs could not defend their opposition to the Afghan war on grounds of conscience.

It would probably be unfair to blame the Chief Whip personally for this comment as she would certainly have been told to say what she did, because the government must by now be very worried indeed at the growing popular and parliamentary hostility to the bombing of the poorest country in the world by the richest.

New Labour appears to want total obedience to the leadership whatever policies it adopts, regardless of whether parliament or the party have given their support. It would like to forbid anyone with doubts from expressing their feelings in the media.

It now appears that the Millbank Tower has started to modernize the Ten Commandments and 'Thou shall not kill' has been amended, by adding 'except when the government orders it'. During the last world war conscientious objectors were excused from military service if they could satisfy a tribunal that their objections were genuinely conscientious, but now that right is being withdrawn from those who speak for peace. Indeed, those who are against the war are now being charged with being of the same ilk as the pre-war Tories who appeased the Nazis. This is a gross distortion of the truth, and I am reminded of the fact that during the Suez aggression by Anthony Eden in 1956 we were also told that President Nasser was another Hitler, in order to justify the attack on Egypt.

It takes a lot of courage for anyone to stand up against this sort of pressure, but happily this does not seem to have deterred Paul Marsden, Jeremy Corbyn, Alan Simpson, Tam Dalyell, George Galloway, or the other principled MPs, and it should not frighten us either.

The longer the war goes on, the more appalling it all becomes, with desperate refugees fleeing from the bombing and facing starvation or death in the cruel winter just ahead, unable to escape because the frontiers are closed and if they try to cross them they risk being shot at by the guards. The casualties among civilians in Afghanistan caused by the bombing, as reported in the media, is already shifting opinion in Britain against the war, and the aid agencies warn that a million or more refugees may die this winter.

There has even been a denunciation of the peace campaigners for being emotional – as if we were able to watch this unfolding tragedy without any feelings of sympathy for the victims or horror at the air-strikes and the casualties they cause. It is always risky to predict the future, but, quite apart from the moral issues raised by the war, it is far from clear that this whole project can possibly succeed militarily. The Israeli occupation of Palestinian towns, and the clear hint that the assassination of Yasser Arafat may be being planned, could well lead to a collapse of the shaky coalition so painfully assembled to support the war.

And the statement by Bush that he has already ordered the CIA to assassinate bin Laden makes a complete non-sense of the claim that the war is to defend democracy and the rule of law, since a fair trial would now be impossible if, by chance, bin Laden were to be captured.

It is all a sombre reminder that states are the main ter-rorists, as when the American government had Patrice Lumumba assassinated and tried to do the same with Fidel Castro and Gaddafy, just as Eden attempted to have Nasser killed in 1956. Looking back on the sanctions against Iraq, it is hard not to see them as a war crime against a people who were in no way responsible for what Saddam Hussein has done.

It would be much more honest to admit that the war currently being waged against Afghanistan has more to do with the White House seeing the growing radicalization of the Arab world as a threat to its global interests than any-thing to do with humanitarian concerns. Imperialism has always been cloaked with false morality in order to win public support for its cause. Older readers of the *Morning Star* will recall that when Britain ruled the world it was just the same. Generations of young people in school were taught to believe that those British troops sent around the world to conquer Asia and Africa were carrying 'the white man's burden'. Thus conquest was presented as a semi-sacred mission to save the 'poor ignorant natives' from their plight and raise them up, when in actual fact we were robbing them of their land and their resources and forcing them to buy British goods, just as today Afghanistan is needed to pipe oil from the Caspian Sea to the West.

All these events which raise moral questions of the highest order quite properly concern all decent people here, including those who were deeply shocked by the atrocity in New York on September 11, and the knowledge that their own views are being faithfully reflected in parliament should be a source of pride and not an occasion for arm-twisting by the Whips.

This is why the huge peace demonstrations around the country are so important, and why we should all support them.

26 October 2001

Progressive politics after New Labour

On Tuesday, Philip Gould, New Labour's chief guru, was speaking at the launch of David Butler's book on the general election before an audience made up mainly of lobby correspondents, academics, researchers and a handful of MPs. He described the way in which the publicity campaigns he has masterminded have changed over the years, ending with the prediction that Labour would be promoting the idea of participation in future elections and encouraging people to realize what fun they are – without mentioning a single political issue that might actually interest the voters.

Participation – as defined by the party managers – is obviously the new buzz-word for the pollsters, focus groups and spin-doctors who have worked so hard to destroy party democracy and establish the tight central control we now see. They are now beginning to realize that all this has entirely failed to inspire those it was supposed to be representing.

If there had been an opportunity to ask Gould a question I would have been tempted to enquire whether, if at all, MPs or Cabinet ministers would be encouraged to participate in the new politics as defined by the masters of the Millbank Tower.

The answer to the question has already been given in parliament, where Labour MPs – with a very few honourable exceptions – have voted overwhelmingly in support of the new Anti-Terrorism Bill which the Home Secretary has introduced. This bill allows the imprisonment of foreigners without a jury trial and so provides for the repeal of Habeas Corpus, which was won years ago and is the foundation of any system of justice.

Any remaining doubts about the role of the Cabinet in policy-formation, debate and decision was dealt with in last Saturday's BBC programme, in which Mo Mowlam made it clear that the Cabinet, like the House of Commons, has been downgraded to the role of ultra-loyal spectator whose only function is to observe the activities of the Prime Minister and cheer him on, whatever he does.

Reading the report of the debate on David Blunkett's Anti-Terrorism Bill I began to wonder whether if ministers chose to dismantle our democracy altogether in the interests of national security there would be more than a handful of Labour MPs who would vote against it. These thoughts have been passing through my mind especially since the general election and the outbreak of the war against Afghanistan, which parliament has never been asked to authorize, or even to support in a proper vote.

The task of this generation is to rebuild our democratic institutions from the bottom up, and then carry that process forward internationally into our economic and industrial life and entrench our rights in a proper constitution that cannot be swept aside so easily.

That is why the massive demonstration in Hyde Park and Trafalgar Square on Sunday was so important, because it was clear that all those who had come were united to do just that and could not be bought off, or frightened away by threats from the bigwigs. It was one of the most exciting political events I can remember, made up of a wide range of people from all over the world: women and men, young and old, along with trade unionists, Muslims, Christians and Jews, and individual members from the Labour, Socialist and Green parties united in opposing the bombing and the war – but also calling for united action on many other fronts.

No one should be discouraged by the attempt to downgrade the scale of the attendance. The police always come up with phoney figures and the media always publicize them in order to give the impression that it was an unrepresentative minority and not a mass movement in the making – which is exactly what it was.

We desperately need an international peace movement, strong in every country and with firm links across the world, and that is now in the making and should be the focus of all our efforts, using all the new means of communication that are now available. It has to be non-violent, as was Gandhi's movement in India, as strong as Mandela's ANC was in South Africa, as determined as Martin Luther King's Civil Rights movement was in America, and as democratic as only we can make it, because we have to do it ourselves and not be looking for charismatic leaders who will take charge and then expect everyone else to cheer them on from the sidelines.

Looking back on last Sunday, there may be lessons that have a wider application to our understanding of the political process and how we should approach it. Perhaps we should mobilize to bring pressure on whatever government is in power rather than putting all our efforts into electoral campaigns, necessary as they are, which can lead to disappointment and sectarianism.

Multinational corporations don't bother to put their people into parliament because they can exercise their influence directly on ministers. The same goes for the banks and the media, which suggests that there may be a parallel for progressive movements using their numbers to get a hearing and so to get results.

This is not quite the docile, harmless and fun-loving participation in politics that Philip Gould is thinking about, but it would certainly be more effective in getting results.

23 November 2001

Tax and spend

The Prime Minister will go down in the history books as the man who created two new political parties, and abolished another political party – which is no mean achievement. First he invented 'New Labour', then he renamed the Labour Party which elected him as its leader as 'Old Labour'. By doing so he seems to think that the Labour Party itself has actually disappeared, although he was re-elected to parliament in June as the Labour Party candidate.

These manoeuvres have only had one purpose: to distance himself from the trade unions, from socialism and from the record of his predecessors as Labour leaders who became prime minister. Above all he is determined that Britain will never go back to a policy of 'tax and spend', which he believes would alienate Rupert Murdoch and Middle England, both of whom he depends upon for support – that strange combination of the *Sun* and those living in the Home Counties who elected Mrs Thatcher three times and who, the spin-doctors believe, will back him now only if he can show himself to be continuing her policies.

All governments tax and spend, and the real question is: who pays the taxes and what are they spent on? If that is not discussed then the whole argument is meaningless.

If pensioners pay through VAT on the necessities which they buy in the shops, and the money raised goes on Trident, that is wrong; but if the wealthy are taxed at a higher rate so as to fund the NHS to provide care for the elderly, that is right.

There is always plenty of money for war and, since New Labour came to power, it has bombed Iraq, former Yugoslavia and Afghanistan, and paid the bill, but pensioners (many of whom served in the forces in the last world war against fascism) are still denied an increase in their pension, in line with earnings. The government would (no doubt) respond to this by saying that defence is in the national interest and you cannot count the cost in time of war. However, we must ask whether those wars were morally right, and what else is also in the national interest which we are currently neglecting.

Most people expect a Labour government to regard the national interest as including health, education and care of the sick and the old, and to fund these services by taxation based upon the ability to pay, rather than leaving them to market forces.

In 1948 the Ministry of Health issued a leaflet to introduce the new National Health Service, which came into existence on 5 July that year. The opening paragraph described it quite clearly under the heading 'What is it? How do you get it?'

> It will provide you with all medical, dental and nursing care. Everyone – rich or poor, man, woman and child – can use it or any part of it. There are no charges, except for a few special items. There are no insurance qualifications. But it is not a 'charity'. You are all paying for it, mainly as taxpayers, and it will relieve your money worries in times of illness.

All prescriptions, all dental care, all spectacles, and even wigs, were absolutely free – this at a time when the nation was still suffering the immense damage done during the war, but it showed that the will to act was there and it was the greatest thing done by that Labour government.

It was also Labour which made grants available for those who went on to college. The introduction by this government of loans and fees has already discouraged some young people from going into higher education for fear of landing up with a huge debt hanging like a millstone around their necks in later life.

And Labour it was, when Barbara Castle was in charge of Social Security, which linked pensions with earnings, funded by a combination of taxation and National Insurance.

Yet now private companies, whose prime responsibility is to their shareholders, are being brought in to run our schools and hospitals. Taxpayers are to be asked to pay for the profits which go to those shareholders instead of the money going directly back into teachers' or nurses' pay or towards funding new equipment.

In 'New Labour's' last manifesto a pledge was given – as in 1997 – that wealthy people would not be asked to pay more income tax, whereas pensioners are subjected to a means test under the minimum pension guarantee.

I hope that the new, and long overdue, debate, opened up after the Chancellor's statement last week, about the need for tax increases to fund our public services does indicate a real change of heart by the government, which would win wide public support.

I also hope that ministers can be persuaded to abandon the hideous practice of 'naming and shaming' those public services that do have problems and need to improve their own performance. The way to help them to do this is to listen to those who work in them, see that the necessary funds are available and give some encouragement instead of attempting to humiliate them in public, which is bound to lower morale and make things worse.

And I am waiting for some public comment by a minister about those private companies which have failed the nation but which are never, never publicly named or shamed. This government wants to be seen as business-friendly and presumably cannot ever criticize the private sector in case it undermines public confidence in the privatization of our public service – a policy which no real Labour government would ever support.

7 December 2001

New Labour abandons comprehensive education

The government's new education policy, which includes more privatization, more selection, more faith schools and the erosion of the role of Local Education Authorities (LEAs) represents a complete reversal of the position taken by socialists in the Labour Party since before the second world war.

From the time that the National Association of Labour Teachers was founded and argued its case with the 1945 Labour government through the Campaign for Comprehensive Education, the Socialist Education Association and beyond, Labour has always argued for comprehensive schools and a fully comprehensive education that would allow all pupils to attend schools where a complete range of subjects would be available.

The unfairness of the eleven-plus has long been recognized by parents across the political spectrum, and in 1965 Tony Crosland, then Minister of Education, invited LEAs to prepare plans for its abolition. Progress was slow but sure, and it was when Mrs Thatcher was Minister of Education that most grammar schools were abolished under pressure from Tory parents who were furious if their own children were marked down as failures at eleven and denied access to the schools of their choice.

Even after New Labour came into being, the pledge to abolish selection survived, and David Blunkett in a famous conference speech said 'Watch my lips – no selection', though later he said it had been a joke. However, as Secretary of State he introduced legislation that would allow selection by aptitude or ability while Downing Street kept Chris Woodhead on at OFSTED and followed a wholly different policy from the one to which we were committed.

A few days ago a new Education Bill was published which led *The Times* to run a front-page story, 'Labour Ends its 30-year War against Grammars', based on the decision to give even more money to grammar schools if they would assist other schools by taking in some of their pupils. Earlier, the phrase 'bog-standard comprehensive' came out from Downing Street as a term of abuse.

For most Labour people this is viewed as a major betrayal, and so it is, but just saying that does not really reveal what the government has in mind, which is to introduce a totally different principle into our system to prepare us for the demands made by the global economy.

Globalization requires small elites to be educated to run the world, while the rest are just to be trained to obey orders and not ask questions, and that is the role allocated to second-tier comprehensive schools, which are in effect to become secondary moderns for those who fail to get selected by aptitude or ability.

Church schools and schools for other faiths are divisive, as they can easily become the means by which selection is reintroduced, given their generous funding. The situation is made much worse by the fact that in our multicultural society all faiths should be taught in all schools, in order to prepare the new generation for the complex world in which we live.

It is hard to escape the conclusion that the government

does not really want the working class to be educated – an explanation which fits in with its policy of fees and loans. This policy is calculated to discourage many working-class youngsters from going on to college, as they fear that they will end up with massive debts to repay.

Meanwhile, the privatization programme which allows commercial companies to take over some schools, and even replace elected councillors, is also a requirement of the global economy which wants to introduce competitive market criteria into all our public services.

And the restriction of public expenditure required by the Maastricht Treaty, together with the limits imposed by the Central Bank in Frankfurt, have been designed to force the Treasury to seek private funds in place of the public financing of education.

One effect of all this is that we may well be denied the huge increase in public educational funding that will be necessary if we want to have a well-educated electorate able to play a full part in our democracy.

It is clear that the campaign for comprehensive education has got to start all over again. The government's strategy must be exposed for what it is – damaging to our youngsters and to democracy itself. These arguments, if clearly put, will have a very wide appeal as a policy for extending to the new generation that opportunity their parents never had.

The government has presented its policy as being in favour of excellence. This sounds fine, but in reality means that the best schools will be reserved for the wealthy and those who have been classified as specially gifted – which really means schools for the children of specially gifted parents.

New Labour has really let us all down. We are being modernized back to the old and discredited policy of the wartime coalition which came out with the theory that there were three sorts of minds – the academic, the practical and the rest. That is how the tripartite system with three types of school and selective exams at the age of eleven came to be introduced.

Unless this policy is challenged and changed our children and grandchildren will suffer. A strong campaign is now needed to mount that challenge and protect the interests of future generations.

14 December 2001

How we are governed now

We should all be supporting the police in their current disagreement with the Home Secretary, who is attempting to impose new pay scales which have been predictably presented as a necessary piece of 'modernization'.

It should now be obvious to everybody that the words 'modernization' and 'reform' are simply being used to justify an attack on the public services and public servants, who can then be presented by the spin-doctors as being obstructive and uncooperative, maybe even opening the way for Securicor to be asked to undertake police duties and cut costs by paying lower salaries and providing a poorer service.

Will the Fire Service find that it too has to face competitors, as happened in the old days when insurance companies provided fire cover and affixed plates to the houses they had insured, so that the company fire appliance could see which houses had to be saved and which were not covered and could therefore be allowed to burn?

But when are we going to hear about reforms to company law to deal with the gross abuse of trust by some corporations whose directors line their own pockets before an announcement is made that there has been a bankruptcy and thousands of workers are to be laid off?

The official view from Downing Street seems to be that everything in the private sector is automatically better and more efficient, despite all the evidence that suggests the opposite is true. Even when workers in a private company do well, as the Dyson workers did with their excellent bagless vacuum cleaner, this does not protect jobs. (The Dyson plant moved to Malaysia where wages are far lower, leaving many of those who designed and built the appliance on the dole.)

There seems to be no moral basis in New Labour policy abroad, since both sides in the Congo civil war are receiving weapons made in Britain – a decision justified on the grounds that it safeguards British jobs. Moreover, after the Prime Minister appealed for peace in Kashmir on a recent visit, it turned out on his return that a massive arms deal had been done there.

Nor is there much consistency, since the Foreign Secretary demands sanctions against Zimbabwe on the grounds that the elections were not fair, but no word is spoken about sanctions against Saudi Arabia or Oman, where they do not have any elections of any kind – but Britain cannot object because they have oil and Zimbabwe does not.

It is hard to believe that any of these decisions were

fully discussed and taken by the Cabinet, for no serious Labour minister could fail to understand all this – and the conclusion must be that the Cabinet does not get to discuss these matters at all, but sits there and is told what has been decided, or maybe only learns about it in the newspapers, as we all have to do. Indeed, I am not sure that we have a functioning Cabinet at all, since the Prime Minister has gathered around him a mass of so-called advisers who were neither elected nor have passed through the rigorous civil service selection system, but who nevertheless have far more power than the Cabinet itself.

Those MPs who have been made Cabinet ministers have become mere advisers themselves, apart from discharging the ritual function of heading up the departments and taking the rap if anything goes wrong, leaving policy to the real Cabinet which the Prime Minister has chosen from amongst his friends. In short, parliamentary democracy and Cabinet government have been quietly abandoned in favour of a king and his courtiers, sustained by ministers and MPs who are expected to fall into line or get the chop, almost as if we have a president without even a House of Representatives to keep him in check.

There are, of course, a number of good MPs who are doing an excellent job in the Commons, and many others who are uneasy about individual policies, but those who do speak out are either ignored or denounced by a media that desperately wants to retain the confidence of those in Downing Street who control the flow of news upon which they themselves depend to retain their jobs. Given that tight control of power and information, the only way we shall ever achieve anything now is by mounting massive campaigns to bring pressure to bear on No. 10, so that even the pollsters and spin-doctors begin to notice and recommend a change of course.

Remote as all that may sound, those who have followed that line have succeeded in getting some policy changes made, as we saw this week with the new line coming from the top that taxes might have to rise to pay for the NHS. For years that option was dismissed as impossible and backward-looking, but now the message has got across the tune is changing and we may get what we have needed for years.

The environmental movement has already had some impact by following the same policy of campaigning, and the principled and determined opposition to privatization by the trade unions could also lead to a rethink on environmental issues. Indeed, a determined peace movement might even frighten off the Prime Minister from supporting another war against Iraq which would be strongly opposed by many who are in no way political.

'Keep up the pressure' would be a good slogan for May Day 2002, and if it is taken up we could start to make real progress.

1 March 2002

The danger of apathy

Apathy is now one of the main talking points of the political classes. They write and broadcast about it all the time, especially with respect to young people, who, they argue, just will not turn up to vote as responsible citizens should, blaming them for the problem.

Certainly the vote is an important right won by earlier

generations, many of whom gave their lives to win what we now take for granted. Indeed, in very recent times black South Africans fought like tigers to gain that right against their previous exclusion from the democratic process by the apartheid regime.

But why, we might ask, are people uninterested in politics – as indeed many are? We must try to understand why the vote seems to have lost so much of its appeal. It seems that there are two reasons why this is happening. First, whereas the political problems facing this generation are challenging, difficult and interesting, the practice and coverage of politics is shallow, abusive and personalized, and that alone is enough to put us off, since exchanges of insults in parliament, the control freakery of the Millbank Tower apparatchiks and the organized punch-ups masterminded on 'Newsnight' simply do not satisfy our desire to know what is going on, why and what we can do about it. The second reason is much deeper, and it is the widely held suspicion that the government itself is apathetic about many of the concerns of those who voted Labour in the last two general elections – a view shared by pensioners facing a cutback in their retirement income and students who cannot understand why they are being asked to pay for their education at college.

People are told that we have to be careful about public expenditure to avoid endangering our economy, but there is always plenty of money about to pay for wars in Iraq, Yugoslavia and Afghanistan. There also seems to be plenty of cash for the boards of directors in British business: for their salary boosts, share options and golden handshakes when they fail. Indeed, they can live happily in the knowledge that they are not going to be asked to pay a penny more on tax at the top rate.

The government is also believed to be apathetic about the ever-widening gap between rich and poor, both here and world-wide, where that gap can be clearly attributable to the injustices that flow from globalization which New Labour supports uncritically. And the government is clearly apathetic about the UN Charter, following Washington into any war they want to wage, whatever the Charter says about international law.

Post Office workers feel that the government is apathetic about the 30,000 jobs that may be lost if the privatization plans for the GPO go ahead, the police feel the same when they face worsened conditions under the plans the Home Secretary is introducing and the teachers cannot understand why they have been singled out for an attack by the Education Secretary.

Labour members feel the government is apathetic about the party and their policy role at conference, while special advisers with no connection to the party are hired to invent policies for No. 10 to consider and approve – a process that has led the BBC to decide that it will no longer televise our conference because they know it has no power.

Many Cabinet ministers too must now being feeling that the Prime Minister is apathetic about them. Loyal Labour MPs are beginning to wonder exactly what role they now play in the business of government, since the key parliamentary committees are not even allowed to cross-examine the government's top advisers.

In short, the government has consciously decided to cut itself off from those it was elected to represent, but still demands that they vote loyally when the time comes without expecting to play any role in policy-making at any other time.

These are very serious weaknesses that we have to correct if we are ever to reclaim the democratic rights which the pioneers fought so hard to give us. These are quite plainly being systematically withdrawn under the guise of 'modernization', but in fact the whole process, and the thinking behind it, is a throwback to a monarchical style of government when the courtiers picked by the king hovered round the throne and were contemptuous of the common people.

The question we have to ask ourselves is, how do we respond to all this? There are many alternatives on offer, including the dream of a new pure socialist party to replace Labour and remedy all the faults that I have described, and there are many honest, decent and sincere people who are working to bring that about. However, we cannot wait for our political system to be completely restructured, though it could possibly happen at some time in the future, and, if it does, New Labour will be the catalyst that brought it about.

What we have to do now is to build public support for radical policies that meet the needs of all those who feel the government is apathetic about them. That points to huge national campaigns like the one on peace which brought 20,000 to Hyde Park and Trafalgar Square last Saturday, and which was absolutely ignored by the media (except of course the *Morning Star*), proving to my satisfaction that the press proprietors and broadcasting bosses are quite happy to see us apathetic about politicians so long as we listen to their pundits and believe what we are told.

That is why we must rediscover our right to participate

in our future and not accept the role allocated to us – as mere spectators of the activities of our leaders who claim the right to take all the decisions and expect us to obey them.

8 March 2002

The cult of consultants

One of the most powerful weapons now used by business against labour is the management consultant, brought in, we are always assured, only to recommend ways of improving efficiency and productivity. However, the real purpose of the consultant is often to downsize, outsource work to others and to invent reasons to lay off those who are employed by the company that has taken them on. This practice of bringing in consultants has grown steadily over the years and is now spreading to the public sector as well, being used as an excuse to break down and privatize operations that have been controlled by democratically elected local authorities, public agencies and even government departments.

A consultant's report can always be presented as being completely objective, since it comes from those who bring special expertise to the job and, being independent, can be trusted to give advice that is not available inside the organization. In practice, many firms bring in consultants to provide them with arguments for doing what they want to do anyway, and the consultants know this very well and make sure, before they start, exactly what is required of them. They will carefully check their recommendations with the management that has engaged them before they submit them to the directors who will then be able to endorse them to their own workforce who are expected to go along with what is proposed.

We have long seen the effect of this in industry, and no doubt it was on the advice of consultants that Dyson decided to close his British factory, making the successful bagless vacuum cleaners, and transfer the work to Malaysia where wages are far lower. Presumably Marconi and Enron too had looked for outsiders to help them to succeed, along with other companies that audit their accounts.

The outsourcing of jobs previously done by staff employed in-house can, on the advice of consultants, be steered towards companies with which the consultant already enjoys a special relationship. Where the consultants are actually asked to follow up their own recommendations within the company, they have power without real responsibility in the organization.

The main gains of outsourcing to those who suggest it is, of course, that the threat of putting work out to tender can be used to worsen conditions for existing staff. If work is actually put out then those employed to do it may have lower wages, poorer working conditions and be less protected from redundancy. This was the case when hospital cleaning contracts went out, often lowering the standard of cleanliness necessary for staff and patients alike.

It is high time that the trade union movement challenged this whole philosophy and rediscovered the case for industrial democracy which would give those who actually do the work the chance to get the information they require, discuss and decide for themselves how the work that they do could be more efficient and what they need, and expect, from their own management.

Many years ago, when in Cuba, I visited a fine hospital in Havana. It was explained to me that every month there were three meetings: one chaired by the management and attended by the unions and the Ministry of Health; the next chaired by the unions, attended by the management and the ministry; and the third chaired by the ministry with management and unions present. All the meetings looked at how the hospital was doing from three different perspectives.

The British Labour movement has a fine tradition of arguing for greater industrial democracy, as, for example in 1910 when Thomas Straker, the secretary of the North-umberland miners, in evidence recommending public ownership of the pits, to the Sankey Commission said:

> Any administration of the mines under nationalization must not leave the miner in the position of a mere wage-earner, whose sole energies are directed to the will of another . . . he must have a share in the management of the industry . . . he must feel that the industry is run by him to produce coal for the use of the community, instead of profit for a few people.

The Union of Post Office Workers, now a part of the CWU (Communications Workers' Union) had the same commitment. With the far higher level of education, technical knowledge and understanding that there is today it must be obvious that the knowledge and skills aquired in-house far exceed those which can be imported by this new breed of management consultants who seem to hover like vultures above us and tell us what to do, entrapping us all in a nightmare of bureaucracy that is both inefficient and destructive of our own powers of imagination and capacity to innovate.

Nor would this in any way threaten the genuine management expertise that exists in-house, for most workers respect good managers and want to support them. In any case, many managers are themselves under threat from the consultants, who may well be undermining their own authority and their jobs too.

At the meeting held last Saturday to launch the campaign to reclaim trade union rights, John Edmonds proclaimed the death of New Labour. He was right to do so, for it is all collapsing around us in a flurry of gimmicks and mutual recrimination. However, all those of us who are looking beyond the present impasse must necessarily be coming up with positive and practical solutions that can also win widespread support; and we must re-establish faith in the contribution the Labour movement can make to benefit those who use the services that are provided, as well as those who actually provide them.

Privatization is the lifeblood of the consultants. We should turn our back on both and believe in ourselves again.

3 May 2002

Where is the Third Way?

New Labour thought it was necessary to have a philosophy to make it look respectable, and that is how the Third Way came to be invented. The same tailor who designed the Emperor's new clothes was approached and produced a suit that served its purpose, at least until Lionel Jospin fell foul of Chirac and Le Pen, and the hard Right seemed to be benefiting from the public sense of disappointment and disillusionment that had set in.

Now we read that the dwindling band of Third Way

devotees are to have a brainstorming session in a stately home to carry the Blair Revolution a stage further. Ex-president Bill Clinton has agreed to come, and will no doubt explain how his own period in power led to the election of George W. Bush.

Those who invented New Labour seem to have concluded that the Tories would never be defeated unless and until we adopted their policies and challenged them on competence in running the economy and offered clean politics to banish sleaze. And that is exactly why New Labour distanced itself from the unions, abolished Clause 4 to make clear its repudiation of socialism and decided to work very closely with big business, drawing many of its policies from the *Daily Mail* and embracing market forces and globalization with such passion that a merger with the Liberals – who share that view – seemed obvious.

This explains the paradox of New Labour's victory in 1997, which was built on the contradiction that the public wanted to get rid of the Tories while the City and Whitehall wanted to safeguard Tory policies under the banner of New Labour, believing that a strong Labour leader, with a loyal party, would be better able to do that than a weak Tory leader with a divided party. A new word had to be invented to cover up what was really happening, and the choice was made quickly – 'modernization' – which allowed all critics to be dismissed as dinosaurs while New Labour was facing the future with confidence.

Of course there have been real achievements, especially in Northern Ireland, with the New Deal, a minimum wage, tax credits and the announcement of plans to boost expenditure in the public services. However, all this has been combined with a massive commitment to privatization, dictated by Brussels, the IMF and the WTO, and the retention of many Tory anti-union laws.

In fact many of these plans, far from modernizing Britain, are throwbacks to the Victorian era, or, as in the case of the House of Lords, a reversion to medieval times when the king picked his favourites on the basis of their loyalty. In foreign policy, we have seen a return to imperialism in the guise of standing shoulder to shoulder with President Bush, whatever he does.

This has led to some confusion, in that Washington and London now describe themselves as the international community, having ditched the UN Charter because it seemed to limit the President's freedom of action. The Bush–Blair axis is simultaneously trying to stop a war between India and Pakistan and start a war with Iraq; condemning Pakistan for its missile tests while planning Star Wars; calling for civil liberties in Cuba while denying them in the US base at Guantanamo Bay, which is a part of Cuba occupied by America.

These absurdities are endless. We blame Mugabe for his election failings, while working closely with Saudi Arabia which has never had an election. We call for a change of regime in Baghdad by force of arms, a change of regime in Venezuela by organizing a *coup d'état*, and a change of leadership in Palestine by endorsing Sharon as a man of peace.

In this country we are told that we must be at the heart of Europe, when in fact many Europeans are strongly opposed to American policy, and that we should prove our commitment to Brussels by joining the euro when not one single country in the euro zone was allowed by its government to decide this question in a referendum.

There is one effect of Third Way politics that everyone

in Britain understands, and that is the growing centralization of political power that has taken place so as to allow the government to get closer to big business, and to Bush and Berlusconi, who are now much more powerful than the party, parliament or the public in deciding what policies are to be followed.

The Cabinet has been reduced to a short weekly staff-meeting for the notification of decisions already taken after discussions with unelected advisers who wield more power than ministers themselves. The House of Commons has been taken for granted and the annual conference has become the platform for a series of ministerial statements, financed by a trade fair where large corporations display their wares and pay real money for the right to do so. The whole top-heavy structure is held together by personal patronage that rewards parliamentary loyalists with high office or a seat for life in the Lords where they sit beside ennobled businessmen.

The proposal for a government-run campaign in a referendum to get us into the euro would undermine our rights even further, because all power would then pass from the MPs we elect and can replace, to commissioners and bankers who we do not elect and cannot remove, which means that they do not have to listen to us or bother about what we want.

This is a recipe for Le Pen, the British National Party, abstention and violence, and that, I fear, is what will happen if Labour follows the lead of those who believe in the Third Way, which could well mean the end of democratic government. We must not let it happen.

31 May 2002

3

Rallies, Dissent and Democracy

The lessons of history

As a Labour MP I live in two quite different worlds that occasionally overlap but often seem not to meet at all.

Parliamentary politics, as reported in the mainstream media, centres almost exclusively on the leading personalities and their relations with each other, the abuse that marks the exchanges between political leaders and the endless stream of slogans designed to market new policy initiatives. But underneath all this elaborate display of top-level activity lies the real world of real people who cannot get their problems, hopes and fears discussed at all, but which reach me through thousands of letters, 'surgery' cases in my constituency and the many public meetings which I attend each month.

In the last few weeks half a dozen such meetings have taken place, each with audiences of up to a thousand. Two of these were demonstrations called to highlight the grave injustice suffered by the Palestinians at the hands of the Israeli government, a policy which enjoys the full support of Washington and London. Among the speakers were Jews, Arabs and socialists.

Two more meetings related to privatization: one in the Central Hall, Westminster, warning of the danger of privatizing council housing; and the other in the Hackney Empire against the cuts being imposed by the Council there.

Another was a big rally in Hammersmith Town Hall on the threat of globalization, at which an American who organized the Seattle demonstration and Boris Kargalitsky from Russia, both spoke. On Monday I attended a meeting about asylum-seekers.

Perhaps the most exciting of all, however, was held in the Dominion Centre in Southall, last Saturday, to celebrate the victory of the Hillingdon strikers, led by Asian women who were victims of the privatization of services there, and who after five years have won a total victory against Pall Mall and Granada. Their victory was achieved against all odds, and for that reason the triumph was all the greater because they won it by courage and persistence, even after their union had withdrawn support for their action.

Apart from the *Morning Star* and the Left press, where could anyone have heard about any of these meetings? The answer is nowhere, because the BBC, ITV and the newspapers are just not interested and regard them as an irrelevance compared with the battle of the giants between party leaders or gossip about arguments within the Cabinet.

Meanwhile, we are told by the great and the good who write their wise and statesmanlike columns in the broadsheets that apathy by the public is the problem, conveniently ignoring the apathy of people at the top about the lives of those they are supposed to represent or whose interests they claim to serve in their capacity as the bold 'free press'.

The danger of this divide is that it is disconnecting people from the political process, thus undermining the whole democratic system, which could well lead to the presentation of these arguments outside as being essentially violent and requiring tough action by the authorities.

All progressive movements have always been denounced as violent in the hope that people will reject them without listening to the arguments. The Tolpuddle Martyrs, the Chartists and the Suffragettes were put in this category, and yet, in the end, their arguments prevailed. Perhaps the most vivid example in recent years is provided by the anti-colonial movement which campaigned for self-determination against the European empires in the postwar years. Mrs Thatcher described Nelson Mandela as a terrorist when he was imprisoned in South Africa, as was Gandhi in India years ago. Then, when the battles were won, they were hailed as leaders in the new Commonwealth. More recently, Gerry Adams was denounced and is now a key figure in the peace process.

For anyone who is serious about social progress, this historical background is absolutely essential, because it helps us to overcome the sustained and professional pessimism that is encouraged by the establishment in order to discourage anyone from carrying on with their campaigns for justice.

But if these campaigns are to succeed, there has to be a better information system available to us, so we can keep in touch with what is happening, here and world-wide, and realize that we are not alone, and here the Internet has great potential.

That is why so many people go to demonstrations, because in a big gathering of like-minded people, we gain confidence and that is why the media don't report them.

The establishment is actually not interested in progressive movements, which they regard as not being newsworthy and they hope, by neglecting them, that those concerned may give up, believing themselves to be voices in the wilderness.

Hope is the fuel of social progress and we can acquire that hope most easily if we remember that throughout the whole of history it has always been the same.

21 March 2001

Campaigning against capitalism

The media coverage of the demonstrations in Canada against the all-American summit on free trade was predictable and misleading, showing violent crowds pitted against riot police without letting us hear what was being said by the many thousands who had gathered to make their case against globalization and the power it gives to big business.

Here in London we are being prepared, in advance, for another orgy of tabloid anger against the anti-capitalist march due on 1 May, with graphic forecasts of the mindless mob violence which we are told we must expect. It is true that some do come to rallies of this kind with the intention of disrupting them, and there might even be a few *agent provocateurs* who have been drafted in by the authorities to discredit the event, as undoubtedly happened at Wapping.

The tactics of police commanders can also make it worse, as we saw in the miners' strike at Orgreave, when it was the cavalry charges by the mounted police which triggered some stone-throwing by pickets. On that occasion through, BBC chiefs instructed the news bulletins to reverse the order of the film in order to suggest that the stones were thrown first and the cavalry charge came second.

The photographers and journalists who will be sent to report on 1 May will all have been instructed to look for any sign of trouble. If a shop window is broken, that will provide the headline, and the constables who face the crowd will be depicted as heroes, without anyone mentioning that the police too are threatened by creeping privatization and may have some sympathy for the demonstrators.

In one sense, the violence, if it happens, will actually be a direct result of the media neglect of serious issues which almost encourages people to throw stones in the hope of getting some attention, even if it is only a studio discussion with a bishop who can be relied upon to 'deplore the irresponsibility of young people stirred up by agitators'.

But the real responsibility for this distortion of the truth lies not with the press and broadcasters but with those political leaders who choose to ignore the real issues raised by the triumphalist arrogance of capitalism which has set its sights on dominating the world and destroying such democratic defences as we have been able to build up over the last century.

The judges may ban a strike by London Underground workers anxious about public safety, but no one even attempted to take Corus to court for sacking thousands of workers in the steel industry, or to hold Motorola to account for their closures in Scotland – both of which have inflicted real and permanent damage on our society.

As a result of all this the most potentially progressive international movements in the world are being deliberately marginalized by the establishment and virtually accused of being terrorists. This has the effect of excluding them from the democratic process and their arguments being ignored.

The socialist and Labour movement here and worldwide must make every effort to reconnect legitimate protest with effective political action by supporting the campaigns against global capital and by explaining what is really going on.

The surest way of eliminating the violence that is born out of despair is to back those who believe that no one is listening and be seen to be working with them to end the injustice that lies behind the anger of the dispossessed. We also owe it to ourselves, and everyone else, to offer some explanation of the nature of globalization, its objectives and its weaknesses, so that we can evolve a realistic strategy for reversing the headlong drift to disaster which will certainly come if we do nothing.

The failure to respond to this challenge is sometimes attributed to the corruption of power which it is widely believed inevitably leads to a betrayal by those at the top, but there is also the parallel problem of the corruption of powerlessness which can persuade those at the bottom to abandon hope of progress, and this can lead to fascism – as we saw in pre-war Europe.

At present the Left is divided, and in the election this division will be revealed when we collect our ballot papers at the polling stations and find that Labour, a variety of socialist and communist candidates are all competing to win our vote.

But after the election is over, when the emptiness of New Labour finally becomes apparent, all socialists and those who are now concentrating on single-issue campaigns, have got to find ways of cooperating, not only on peace, jobs, trade union rights, pensions, and the environment, but also on a wider, and more comprehensive, international educational campaign against capitalism and for democracy and socialism.

25 April 2001

The silent takeover

Sometimes a single event can clarify a complex situation and that is what happened in Sweden last week when the police opened fire on the anti-globalization demonstration. The Prime Minister immediately denounced the demonstrators as an 'anarchist circus' opposed to democracy. The European ministers are apparently considering holding future summits on a warship in the Mediterranean in order to protect themselves.

Compare that reaction with the praise in the British establishment given to the students in Tienanman Square, who were denounced and attacked by the Beijing government, but were hailed here as campaigners for democracy against a repressive regime.

Yet that is exactly what the anti-globalization movement is all about – a popular demand for the democratic control of our own future against the power now wielded by multinational companies, the WTO, the IMF, the European Commissioners and central bankers who now effectively run the world in their own interests.

Noreena Hertz has just published a new book, which is both scholarly and readable, called *The Silent Takeover – Global Capitalism and the Death of Democracy*, which brilliantly describes and analyses exactly what is going on and what it means. She has also written another book, which I have not yet read, called *Russian Business Relationships in the Wake of Reform*, based on her experience while working for the World Bank in Moscow, when she saw at first hand the impact those reforms had upon the Russian people, following the privatization of their industry and services. (She is now the Assistant Director of the Centre of International Business and Management at the Judge Institute of the University of Cambridge, where she obtained her PhD.)

I mention her book just because she has written a clinical account of the process she describes, free from the rhetoric of the Left, which gives it a wider appeal, and also because, being in her early thirties, she cannot be dismissed as Old Labour, indeed her arguments make New Labour look very old-fashioned indeed.

Far from being a threat to democracy, the Seattle movement represents a demand for democracy to allow us to work together for peace and justice and human survival in a planet that could easily be destroyed by a new arms race or even by neglecting our environment.

The contempt for democracy shown by the President of the European Commission was clearly demonstrated when he ignored the Irish referendum vote against the Treaty of Nice and announced that the plans to integrate the EU would go ahead, along with the Rapid Reaction Force rejected by the Irish.

If Britain votes against the euro in a referendum, will our decision be treated with the same contempt and, if so, what would that tell us about our own much-proclaimed democracy? This is not a theoretical question that can be dismissed as concerning only academics and professional dissidents since it will have direct consequences for us all. For example, the decision of the government to privatize health and education stems directly from the policies being advocated both in Europe and by the global corporations, and they are looking to make a lot of money out of it.

That is why, in the *Sunday Times* business section, investors were advised to put their money into seven named companies which specialize in running hospitals and schools, predicting that their shares would soar, and citing one company, which already runs and manages schools, whose profits have actually risen by 50 per cent over the past six months.

And there is a lot more money to be made out of a new arms race, which is what President Bush came to Europe to promote, along with his decision to ditch the Kyoto Treaty which would hit the profits of his friends and backers in industry, upon whom he depends.

These are the very same methods that were used by the hard Right in Europe in the 1930s: identify your critics as subversive, join up with big business, give them power and find a foreign enemy to justify your rearmament. We must not let it happen here, in the name of modernization, globalization or free trade, which is why the demonstrators at Gothenburg deserve our support.

The recent letter signed by several trade union general secretaries opposing Star Wars and other warnings that are coming from the unions at their conferences against privatization are a sign that the trade unions intend to play a larger and more positive role in policy-making in the party than they have done recently, and we must encourage them to take a strong line at Labour's annual conference in Brighton this autumn.

It was the trade unions that saved the party in 1931 when Ramsay MacDonald, then the Labour Prime Minister, entered into a coalition government including Tories and Liberals under pressure from the bankers. I am not saying that that would happen again, but if ever it did, we should need the trade unions to save us again.

22 June 2001

The birth of a world movement for democracy

The demonstrations at Genoa, so bitterly denounced by all the world leaders who attended – and so brutally repressed by the Italian police – will be remembered by future historians as another milestone in the long process of building a global movement for democracy.

Many different groups were represented there from many different countries, each with their own agenda and the media made much of it to discredit them all. But they all had one thing in common – the clear demand to be heard and represented so that they could have some influence over the decisions that will affect our lives in the future.

The violence of a small minority was nothing compared

to the state violence to which they were subjected, and though I believe in non-violence, it has to be admitted that the media would have ignored it had this been a quiet political rally, however big. We do not need lessons on the importance of peace from President Bush who is planning a huge nuclear rearmament programme through Star Wars, or from the Prime Minister who supports the use of sanctions against Iraq which has cost the lives of half a million innocent Iraqi children over the last ten years. Nor should anyone be too ready to listen to pleas for peace from President Putin, after Chechnya, or any NATO members who agreed to the use of depleted uranium in former Yugoslavia.

The other argument that was deployed against the protesters at the summit was that the heads of state claimed to have been democratically elected, and therefore they could claim legitimacy whereas those on the streets could make no such claim. But even that argument needs to be examined in the light of the fact that many of the most powerful forces in the world have not been democratically elected. For instance, the bosses at Ford, General Motors, Toyota, Microsoft and the other multinationals have never been elected, neither has the IMF, the WTO or the World Bank, which, along with the Brussels Commission and the Frankfurt Bank have far more power than most elected governments. Indeed, in America big business funds both political parties and expects a pay-off whichever one wins – a process which is well advanced here and elsewhere in the modern world, and which is why Bush cannot accept the Kyoto agreement on global warming.

Of course technology has long since abolished distance, and there is a need for international institutions to take account of this, but up until now international agreements have been made with little reference to national parliaments. This has resulted in the establishment of completely unaccountable organizations which are not elected, cannot be removed and do not have to listen to the demands of those over whom they have so much power. By contrast, the demand for democracy underpinned the anti-colonial movement and the peace movement's 'No annihilation without representation', and it now inspires the Seattle movement.

The historical parallels with the development of democracy in Britain seem to me to be very close, since in 1832 only 2 per cent of the population had the vote and they were all rich men, which is roughly the same percentage of powerful people who run the world today.

We should also remember that all the advances that have been made have always been marked by bloodshed, because rich and powerful people never give up their wealth or power without a fight, which is one reason why in Genoa the police were authorized to use such disproportionate force.

So if we do want a really democratic world order we must demand that the UN General Assembly be elected by the people in every country, that it is responsible for electing the Security Council itself and that it controls the WTO, IMF and World Bank, and develops an active industrial policy to control the multinationals with power to enforce its decisions. This may sound very idealistic and impractical, but so too were the demands for the vote made by the Chartists, and those made by the African National Congress when it challenged the apartheid regime in South Africa.

It is essential that the anti-globalization movement makes clear and positive demands and does not confine itself to negative protest. In Britain we have to channel some of the energy that now goes into protest back into the ballot box. We have a full century of hard political campaigning ahead of us but thanks to the pioneers at Seattle, Gothenburg and Genoa we have a huge army of supporters now being mobilized across the globe ready to do just that. Sometimes I am overawed by the immensity of the task that awaits us, but I also feel excited by the conviction that it can and will be done.

27 July 2001

Devoting more time to politics

Having left parliament to devote more time to politics I am struck by the ceaseless propaganda against the Left, the trade unions, the peace movement and all those who are campaigning for democracy and human rights – propaganda which certainly has an effect.

A few days ago when I was shopping for a present for an old friend who is eighty, the assistant who helped me said, 'Mr Benn I must tell you that I am New Labour because I don't want to see the trade unions running the country ever again.' The man who said it was a young Asian, and if he ever experiences any sort of racial harassment, or loses his job when the business where he works closes down, he might discover that it would be the trade unions who would be defending him and his family.

Then there was the article in the *Independent on Sunday* by Colin Brown, the political editor, who wrote that John

Prescott has 'come out fighting against the union leaders who are threatening to disrupt Labour's annual conference over private finance for schools, hospitals and the London Underground'.

Our annual conference is a place where we debate our policy and vote on it, and this democratic process is now described as disruptive – implying that the unions intend to wreck something, like those who threw stones at Genoa.

Recently the German Interior Minister Otto Schily suggested that the European Union should form an EU riot squad to protect the leaders from any disruption at future gatherings, though he did not say whether it should be used at our party conference too to be sure that the Prime Minister had no trouble with the trade unions.

We are now faced with the possibility that electric stun guns may be issued to the police, which would allow them to paralyse trouble-makers who were suspected of taking violent action and temporarily disable them, but presumably they will not be issued at the TUC. No one has yet described parliamentary critics of the government as disruptive, but in the 1930s European fascists did denounce democracy and shut it down.

Reading all this I sometimes do wonder whether we are not heading for a period of right-wing repression to keep us in order and intimidate all those who might consider marching through the streets to get their case across. With these thoughts in mind I went last week to join two completely peaceful demonstrations that took place in the heart of London, only covered, I must add, in the *Morning Star*.

The first was organized by 'Voices in the Wilderness',

which I learned had been founded in the United States in 1998 when the bombing of Iraq began again and this was its sister organization, a reminder of the large number of radical movements against war and globalization that exist in America, but which the British media deliberately ignore, just as the US press ignores our work here.

We marched to Downing Street to present a petition to the Prime Minister, demanding an end to the sanctions against the people of Iraq which have caused untold suffering to the innocent and caused the death of literally hundreds of thousands of children who were denied the treatment that they need. (While we were actually walking down Whitehall, a woman from the BBC rang on a mobile phone to ask me whether demonstrations ever achieved anything, and I told her that she would never have won the vote if the Suffragettes had not demonstrated.)

Among the many who were there was one lady of sixty-six who had actually been in Genoa and told me that the Italian police had attacked her little group of demonstrators, while absolutely ignoring the Black Box anarchists who had been throwing bricks, but are now suspected of having been *agents provocateurs*. Her courage was astonishing, as was the courage of Sue Davis whom I met the following day in Tavistock Square when CND held a short meeting by the tree planted to remember the victims who died at Hiroshima and Nagasaki, and who, as a member of Trident Ploughshares described her experiences when she was arrested.

Bruce Kent was there too, and spoke of his own peace march. Also present was an American professor of religious studies at a college in New York City who told me of his own work for peace and socialism. We walked for nearly an hour and then handed in another letter for the Prime Minister – this time against Star Wars.

The surest remedy for pessimism is action, and when we are amongst those who are actually doing something it washes away the sense of isolation that the British establishment tries so hard to create, in the hope of persuading us that those who want a better world are all dangerous, unrepresentative and bound to fail.

Having been driven in a ministerial car to weekly Cabinet meetings at No. 10, for over ten years, it feels very good to be outside again, especially when my comrades were demanding what the world needs and wants most – a chance to live in peace.

I'm very glad to have gone back into politics.

17 August 2001

Public meetings

The BBC and ITV seem to have a policy that no public meetings are to be reported, unless they lead to trouble, in which case they are covered with dramatic pictures of the police in action against some 'troublemakers' and the ritual denunciation of the violence by some minister.

All we usually see of a peace demonstration on TV news is a man in a George Bush rubber mask, an angry shouting bearded Muslim and a few young people with posters, but we are never allowed to hear what is said from the platform. The only exception to this that I can think of was when the Countryside Alliance held their big demonstration in London in support of fox-hunting, where a few clips were shown of some Tory front-bencher warning that the rural areas could not survive unless the gentry could continue to practise their barbaric blood-sport.

But strike meetings, which are now going on around the rail disputes have had no coverage, nor have the mass of gatherings, large and small, which go on and have gone on for years in and around the issues which matter to the Labour movement, and it must be because the TV pundits do not want those views to get through to the public.

There is, I suspect, another reason which is more human, namely that the top-rank media commentators do not want to share their God-given right to address the nation and tell us what to think, with anyone who is not a superstar, and even when people are interviewed they are always told to look away from the camera for fear that if they spoke facing it directly it might have too much impact.

Most viewers and listeners therefore never hear about public meetings, and so the media tell us that public meetings are a thing of the past, as I discovered recently when I was invited by the BBC to do a programme on the death of the public meeting. However many times I tried to tell them about the number that I personally attend, they still persisted with their obituaries.

Maybe the tradition of the old hustings at election time has been replaced by party political broadcasts, but as any active member of any progressive organization will tell you, meetings allow important issues to be raised publicly. That is how the Poll Tax was beaten and the mass meetings against the Afghan War brought together those who were opposed to it, and the environmental movement used them to get Green issues on to the political agenda.

During the miners' strike in 1984–85 huge meetings were held all over Britain and other countries in their support, and the funds raised helped to keep the families going, as they did in the case of the Liverpool dockers. In both disputes the women from the support groups made brilliant speeches which I shall never forget.

The annual Durham miners' gala is an inspiration, attended by thousands from the mining families, joined nowadays by trade unionists with their banners from all over Britain, and, until Neil Kinnock stopped going, always attended by the Labour leader who spoke to the crowds on the racecourse about the movement and socialism, to remind us of where we all came from.

The biggest public meeting at which I ever spoke was in 1960 in Bombay, alongside Pandit Nehru and Krishna Menon, against the Portuguese occupation of Goa; it was attended by half a million people. But even in this country, 100,000 people turned out in Trafalgar Square last November to make known their feelings about the war plans against Iraq.

Nor should we forget the role of folk music in keeping alive popular traditions at festivals all over the country, where singers like Roy Bailey remind us of the struggles of past generations and keep our spirits up. This is why an interest in folk music was noted by the Un-American Activities Committee at the time of the infamous McCarthy witch-hunts, as an indication of those who might be political subversives.

Of course many meetings are much smaller, as they were last Sunday, when a hundred people stood in the pouring rain at the Battersea cemetery, listening to speeches commemorating the life of John Burns, one of the first working men elected to parliament in 1892 as a Labour candidate, alongside Keir Hardie.

Later that afternoon the Irish Centre in Hammersmith was packed to the doors to discuss Bloody Sunday. Some brilliant speeches were made, while outside the police kept an eye on a small disconsolate group of youngsters with Union Jacks, who might even have been convened by the National Front.

Some, in New Labour, speak contemptuously of meetings as preaching to the converted, but even if that were true – which it is not – they ought to know that the Christian religion has been kept alive for centuries by doing just that in tens of thousands of churches across the world, and if, instead, the Pope relied upon a few photo-opportunities when there was a miracle at Lourdes he would have no influence at all.

Of course it would be great if the media reported our meetings so that a wider audience could hear what is being said, but even if they did, it would be no substitute for the self-confidence we all get from attending them, not only to hear the speakers, and sometimes heckle them, but because with a big crowd we realize that we are not alone in our faith and can draw strength from the others who have come along to demonstrate their own deep commitment and determination – which is the key to success for the cause now, just as it was for the pioneers.

World-wide, people are also demonstrating for peace and social justice and their cause is our cause too.

1 February 2002

The Levellers and Labour history

Last Saturday a large crowd of people gathered in Burford, to remember three Leveller soldiers: Cornet Thompson, Corporal Perkins and Private Church who refused to serve in Ireland and were shot in the churchyard on the orders of Oliver Cromwell.

For the last 27 years the Oxford WEA (Workers' Educational Association) has been organizing these events and inviting speakers down, parading with bands and banners through the town, followed by the laying of a wreath with their names inscribed on it in the churchyard, the whole event enlivened by Morris dancers and men and women dressed up as Cromwellian soldiers, wearing the green which was the colour they adopted.

This year it was raining, but the people who had come were content to ignore the weather and listen to the speakers including Lindis Percy, a woman twelve times imprisoned for her courageous and imaginative campaign against Star Wars, who argued with knowledge and passion, followed by two other women and Bruce Kent. Listening to them was most inspiring, and nearby were stands put up by Amnesty, Oxfam, Greenpeace and a host of other progressive organizations which keep the flame of hope alive at a time when it is so easy to get depressed and feel that there is nothing we can do to reverse the trend to disaster which so often seems to overwhelm us.

During the English Revolution some important debates about democracy took place in Putney Church, and next Tuesday, on BBC Radio 4, these are being re-enacted, together with a discussion about their relevance today, for the issues raised, which were hotly argued over at the time, sound very contemporary to this generation, since both King Charles I and Cromwell, in his role as Lord Protector, both believed that they had a divine right to rule and would not tolerate dissent.

The older I get, the more convinced I am that no one in power ever wants to share it, and that even progressive regimes that have got control, whether by revolution or election, soon succeed in persuading themselves that all criticism is disruptive or disloyal, made by extremists or wreckers who must – in the public interest – be restrained or removed.

Kings, queens and dictators have always taken that view, and so did the bishops in the days when the churches had real power, being quite happy to burn heretics who undermined their authority. Unhappily, Stalin's Russia did the same in the name of defending the working class from their class enemies, suppressing dissent which denied them the base in public support for socialism that it needed to survive.

The archives of the Labour movement, which chronicle the work and faith of a succession of progressive people in this country who fought for human rights, trade unionism, democracy and peace, are to be found in the Public Record Office in Kew. Occasionally these archives are put on display, so that we can appreciate how much effort and sacrifice went into the task of winning us such rights as we now have. But if you ask where and how such a supreme collection came to be assembled, they will tell you that they all came from the Home Office – i.e. the police records meticulously collected so that 'subversive activities' could be carefully monitored, and they include leaflets, posters, pamphlets and notes of speeches made to the crowd by 'agitators'.

On a recent visit there, speaking at the annual meeting of the PCS union, I was shown the court judgment of the King's Bench Division in the case of Joseph Wilkinson, a textile worker, who, in 1724, was imprisoned for taking part in a strike. This was then an offence because it was in restraint of trade, and the evidence which was the basis of his conviction was that he was a member of a friendly society which was the forerunner of the modern trade union.

Today that process of surveillance still goes on, but even more intensely using the most modern technology which allows the security services to use CCTV, bug anyone they wish to bug and intercept emails, letters and all communication for the purpose of controlling us in the interests of those in power, justifying it all in the interests of 'national security'.

All this makes it so necessary for us to study our history so that we come to understand the reasons why, over the centuries, rich and powerful people want to control us and keep us in our place so that we cannot challenge their privileges by demanding representation and democracy. The knowledge that we are not the first generation to have experienced this pressure from above should give us the confidence to carry on.

The Levellers declared that 'the Earth is a Common Treasury and it is a crime to buy and sell the Earth for private gain', which was the forerunner of the modern environmental movement and they were punished for saying that, just as in the early eighteenth century Joseph Wilkinson was sent to gaol for going on strike and in our own time Lindis Percy was imprisoned for campaigning against Star Wars.

But just as the authorities have more sophisticated ways of watching us, so we have the experience of centuries of work behind us. Moreover, the Internet allows us to internationalize the struggles so that we are able to feel less isolated. History is a real and powerful resource, available for us today; we must make the effort to learn it and use it to get our case across to a people who are waiting to hear from us how they can best make use of their own experience to meet their own needs, and to realize their dreams by working with others to safeguard the democratic rights that global capital would like to take away.

24 May 2002

The Left in America

One of the most dangerous examples of censorship in the media is the virtual absence in our newspapers and on television of any serious reporting of the activities of the Left in America, and many people assume that almost all Americans support President Bush and his policies, which were discussed, last weekend, at a conference in Washington organized by the International Democrat Union (the thinktank of the world's Right).

Since I got connected to the Internet I have been receiving a stream of e-mails from *portsidemod@yahoo.com*, which, at least ten times a day, sends me information about the American Left which is both intensely interesting and very encouraging. Over the last few days, three in particular have caught my attention.

The first reported an article by Congressman Bernie Saunders, a socialist member of the House of Representatives, who has written a powerful account of the scale of 'corporate' welfare in the United States; he has calculated that $125 billion a year are paid by the American taxpayer in grants, tax-breaks and subsidies to some of the largest and most profitable corporations, at a time when the United States has an incredible $6 trillion national debt and is actually borrowing money from the Social Security Trust Fund to pay its way.

He cites the Export–Import Bank which issued loan guarantees to Enron, Boeing, Mobil, IBM, General Electric, Motorola and General Motors, amongst others, much of it in so-called job creation schemes to companies that are actually eliminating hundreds of thousands of American jobs by moving plants to China, Mexico, Vietnam or wherever the wages are lower.

Time magazine recently calculated that one-third of a million jobs have gone down the drain over the last ten years, all from companies that have received more than 60 per cent of the Export–Import subsidies, and it is clear that the process of deliberate de-industrialization, which has so damaged our own manufacturing base here in Britain, is also going on apace across the Atlantic in pursuit of Third Way policies necessary to sustain capitalism.

The second e-mail reports on the decision by the Green Party to select Stanley Aronowitz, a sociology professor, former steel-worker, trade union organizer and peace campaigner, to be their candidate for the governorship of New York State. His programme includes, amongst other things, the following policies: high-quality schools, free tuition at universities, state-subsidized health insurance and universal public childcare. All these would be paid for by progressive taxation and there would be an end to tax giveaways for the rich.

The programme goes on to include the closure of nuclear power plants and a move to renewable energy and conservation; subsidies for affordable housing and grants for organic farming to revitalize local economies; a guaranteed income to replace the bankrupt welfare system, allowing for greater help for single mothers, with birth control and abortion advice to be covered by employers' health insurance; and opposition to the curtailment of civil liberties, the attack on immigrants and the austerity programmes which are now justified by the campaign against terrorism.

The third e-mail which caught my eye reported on the decision by the AFL–CIO General Board (America's equivalent of the TUC General Council) to require every affiliated trade unionist to pay four cents a month more, over the next three years, which would generate $17.5 million to fund a campaign.

John Sweeney, the AFL–CIO president, pointed out that one-third of all members of the US Congress were millionaires and that union households make up 26 per cent of the total national vote, distributed 21 million worksite leaflets and sent 15 million mail messages to its members.

The campaigns which the AFL–CIO unions are to run will be centred around a programme called 'Agenda for America', dealing with the state of the economy, unemployment, health insurance, social security and corporate greed, but contain no reference to the war on terrorism, even though the cost of that war explains why life is so difficult for American workers.

A socialist critique of capitalism, a programme of reform geared to help those who need it most and evidence that the US trade unions seem to be serious about their political role is good news for our Labour and socialist movement, reminding me that Keir Hardie believed that America would go socialist before Britain did, in part because he thought it was not weighed down by all the feudal baggage which we have to carry and which we saw on display during the Queen's Golden Jubilee.

It is true that very little of the American Left has yet felt able to take a stand against the imperialist war policies which are the centrepiece of White House thinking, though we can hardly complain since the New Labour government has committed itself totally to those policies, albeit with far less public support than Bush can rely on.

In the long-term it will be the American people, properly informed and well led who must play a key role in ending the US Empire, just as the Left in Britain helped the national liberation leaders to get their case across in Britain, finding good and strong allies here to support their demands.

The Atlantic Ocean may be wide, but *portsidemod@yahoo.com* has helped to narrow it, and with the power of the Internet growing we should not be surprised to hear that the security services have now been authorized to intercept all our e-mail messages because they know that we are stronger than we ourselves seem to realize.

14 June 2002

4

September 11 and its aftermath

After the bombing

The huge tragedy of wholly innocent people caught up in the bombing of New York and Washington has quite properly occupied the attention of everyone in Britain. The messages of sympathy that have been sent are real and moving. No one could ever have imagined that they would see pictures showing such devastation in America, which is by far the most powerful nation the world has ever seen.

We are used to watching television news bulletins showing Hanoi being bombed, or Baghdad or Belgrade, but America we all thought was exempt, and now that has changed and the world will never be the same again. For what was destroyed was not just the World Trade Center and the Pentagon, but the illusion that any nation great or small could act without consequences. The old ideas about defence have been shattered.

Traditionally nations protected themselves from attack by threatening to kill their enemy, but that does not work when you are up against a suicide bomber who is ready to die and take you with him, and however many smart bombs a country may have they don't help either.

It is not hard to imagine a situation in which chemical or biological weapons are smuggled into any country, however well defended, and the assumed supremacy that we associate with industrial muscle and atomic warheads may just be an illusion.

Indeed, one of the surest casualties of this tragedy has been the Star Wars project, which would have been no help at all against such an attack. Whereas if the 60-billion dollar cost of it was diverted to help reduce world poverty that might just help to reduce the risk of conflict.

Predictably President Bush warns of retaliation, but against whom and with what? For no one can be sure who is responsible, and the suicide bombers themselves were engaged in retaliation since they may well have been the sons or brothers of civilians who were killed when Iraq was bombed, as it has been for the last ten years – most recently a week ago.

Osama bin Laden is the suspect most often mentioned, but we are not often reminded that he was trained and financed by the CIA when President Bush's father was in charge of it. Bin Laden was sent to Afghanistan, his headquarters built for him by the Americans, to be a 'freedom-fighter' against the Russians who then occupied that country. In Moscow at the time he was seen as a terrorist, which is how he is now seen in Washington.

After the attacks on the US embassies in Africa three years ago Clinton launched a massive missile attack on a factory in the Sudan, which everyone now knows had nothing whatsoever to do with the original assault. For all I know the suicide bomber this week may have seen what he did this week as a retaliation for that.

There can be no end to revenge killings, and when the

White House advises Israelis and Arabs to call a ceasefire and start peace talks it is right – and maybe they should take their own advice now. Certainly Israel, which has an immensely powerful army itself, is learning that its forces cannot quell the Palestinian intifada, and America too may have to learn that lesson.

The Prime Minister's grave warnings and pledges of full support for the President suggest that if the United States does strike back with force, British planes may be made available to join them. When parliament meets today I hope that the danger of that is spelled out in the debate. It is right that the House of Commons is being recalled, as was the US Congress, because we need to gather experience and wisdom from all over the world if we are to respond in the right way to this tragedy. This is why the UN General Assembly should also meet in an emergency session, in which the real underlying causes of this crisis can be explored.

Whether this situation is going to be made worse by the impending world recession we do not yet know, but anxiety and fear are now widespread and we know from experience that such fear can easily breed hatred and bring far Right governments to power, justifying their authoritarianism by identifying scapegoats who have got to be eliminated.

All this points to the need for serious discussion by serious people, drawn from every continent, avoid escalation. We owe it to the Americans who have suffered, as well as to ourselves and the rest of the world, to think before we take immediate military action that might just escalate into a world conflict that no one can control.

Sometimes good can come out of evil, and maybe the

scenes we have been watching on our TV screens over the last three days will bring people to their senses; but it depends on what we do, too, and there can be no peace without social justice. Labour Action for Peace at its own meeting in London, just after these appalling attacks, strongly warned against US unilateral military retaliation and urged the summoning of a special UN meeting to discuss the international situation as a whole.

I hope the Labour and peace movements take up this call.

14 September 2001

World peace: the next step

As the world waits anxiously after the bombing of New York and Washington, a lot more is going on under the surface than would appear from the media. Sympathy for the innocent victims in the United States has quite properly expressed itself in many statements of support for President Bush, but it is obvious that privately he is being advised by many world leaders not to do anything that could make the situation worse.

The use of the words 'war' and 'crusade' against Islamic fundamentalism, talk about wanting Osama bin Laden 'dead or alive' or 'air-strikes' against Afghanistan do not help. If bin Laden is killed, or handed over to be tried in America and then executed or imprisoned, or if Kabul is completely destroyed by cruise missiles – what will have been achieved beyond escalating the war to new levels of violence?

Our first duty to our American friends is to give good

advice, as Clem Attlee did in 1950 when he flew to Washington to warn President Truman not to use an atom bomb in Korea. And in 1956 President Eisenhower was strongly opposed to Sir Anthony Eden's war of aggression against Egypt at the time of the Suez war, and effectively secured a British withdrawal.

There are some signs that the United States is listening. The Israelis have been told to agree to a ceasefire because a continuation of their attacks on the Palestinians could undermine Arab support for the coalition against terrorism. Similarly, I hope that the White House will realize that the Muslim world will not tolerate the stiffening of sanctions or major air attacks against Iraq after hundreds of thousands of innocent Iraqis have suffered so much.

What is needed are political solutions that can reduce terrorism, as we have learned from Northern Ireland and South Africa, where the underlying problems were tackled directly and acceptable agreements reached that brought some stability.

The international arms trade is itself criminal, selling weapons to anyone for profit. Years ago in Algeria I was told by a former Egyptian Foreign Minister that they had had a seminar in Cairo on the Crusades, and had discovered that the European arms manufacturers had supplied bows and arrows and spears to both the Christian King Richard and to Saladin, the Muslim leader, during that war.

The time has come for the UN General Assembly to be recalled in order to discuss and agree a policy that deals with all the many complex aspects of this issue, including a proper definition of terrorism, the establishment of an independent world court with jurisdiction over all nations – including the United States – covering war crimes and genocide under the rule of law.

The definition of terrorism may prove quite difficult, as many governments would be glad to see any opposition group in their own country branded as terrorist: the Tamils in Sri Lanka; the Kurds in Turkey; Chechnyans in Russia; and even the Falun Gong in China. We must not end up giving all governments new powers over dissidents, endangering civil liberties and so causing more terrorism.

Those who remember the Birmingham Six and the Guildford Four, who were wrongly charged and imprisoned for IRA bomb attacks that they did not commit, should also remember that an outcry for retribution can lead to innocent people being blamed just to satisfy public opinion.

Perhaps our most important job is to prevent despair from spreading, as it did in the 1930s, when Hitler used the sense of hopelessness in Germany – where six million were unemployed – to identify scapegoats and bring jobs back by rearmament, which led to a war costing 50 million lives.

If the world economy, already shaken by fears of a recession, actually takes a downturn because of the uncertainty of war, we could recreate similar conditions. The danger to the ethnic communities here – especially Muslims – is one that we must guard against.

Older people who remember the Blitz and the horrors of war, may recall the hope we placed in the UN when it was set up in 1945, and the words of the preamble to its Charter:

> We, the peoples of the United Nations, determined to save succeeding generations from the scourge of war, which twice in our lifetime has brought untold sorrow to mankind and

to reaffirm faith in fundamental human rights, in the dignity and worth of the human person, in the equal rights of men and women and of nations large and small and

to establish conditions under which justice and respect for the obligations of treaties and other sources of international law can be maintained and

to promote social progress and better standards of life in larger freedom . . . have resolved to combine our efforts to accomplish these aims.

That was the pledge given by my generation to this generation and we must renew that pledge now for our children and grandchildren.

21 September 2001

The international peace appeal

As the crisis deepens, fear itself could prove to be our worst enemy, as it feeds upon itself and encourages all those, on all sides in this developing situation, who believe that the use of force is the only way forward.

What is needed now is the restoration of hope, and who are better able to offer that message than some of the most experienced world leaders who have lived through many crises in the past and learned from them? That is why the initiative has been taken to bring together a group of international statesmen and women who might be prepared to lend their names to an appeal for a special session of the UN General Assembly to be convened to address all the most pressing problems we face. These would necessarily include issues of poverty, disease, the arms trade, disarmament, the environment, exploitation, refugees, the establishment of a Palestinian state and an end to the suffering of the people of Iraq.

If this appeal were to succeed, we would have to gain the backing of a diverse range of individuals and organizations from every continent, each carrying authority in their own countries, raising some of the same questions which have featured in the anti-globalization campaigns.

A great deal has been written about fundamentalism, but the faithful who follow the teachings of Islam, Christianity and Judaism have long been left behind by the strongest religion of all, which is about the worship of money. The banks are now bigger than the churches, mosques and synagogues. Financial experts on TV who chant the Dow Jones and Footsie like hymns to their new God have greater influence than any bishops, mullahs or rabbis. If we do slide into war it will be to protect the wealth and privileges of the rich and powerful from the weak and poor who are demanding justice.

One of the most serious problems we have arises from the complete abandonment of the UN in favour of NATO. Arguments for unilateral action by the United States seem to have no time for the UN General Assembly, while simultaneously pressing for a world-wide coalition against terrorism. The emphasis on the UN, which is an embryonic world parliament, however imperfect, could win a lot of support from nations that do not wish to be sucked in merely as junior partners in any operation run exclusively by Washington.

The most important thing now is to restore a credible hope that these problems can be solved in a way that does not depend solely or mainly upon air-strikes and military action that could serve only to increase tension and intensify the sort of suicide attacks which we saw in New York.

This UN appeal could have a calming effect on public opinion, which knows that something has to be done, but in the absence of an alternative strategy, may be tempted to see bombing as the only way of tackling the problem. The desire for retaliation is very strong, but an escalation could make the situation ten times worse, while we all know, from experience, that some talking somewhere will have to take place.

I am writing this before the latest news has come in, and by the time this article is printed the whole situation may have changed – almost inevitably for the worse, but rather than outdating this appeal it could make it more urgent. The growing peace movement, here, in America and all over the world, needs a focus for our global campaign that can unite our objectives into a simple and intelligible call to everyone to rally round a demand that obviously makes sense. If, for example Mandela, Gorbachev, Carter and Castro did find it possible to unite around this appeal I am certain that it could soon become a rallying cry that no government could ignore and that the mass media would have to report.

The media have a central role, for if all we read, hear and see is about the dispatch of forces poised for action, and the voices for peace are largely censored, it will necessarily deepen the despair, and act as a mobilization for war in the minds of many people. This will then be reported, through opinion polls, in a way which will give government a completely false idea of the popular desire for peace, which must be in the hearts of a clear majority in every country in the world.

This is why the anti-war movement is so important, for if the Palestinians gain a homeland and a state, if the people of Iraq can be spared more suffering, if world debt which cripples the poorest countries can be cancelled and the defence budgets can be redirected towards even more funding for development, then we would all be much safer than air-strikes could ever make us. All those working for peace at the many public rallies and vigils that are now taking place up and down the country, should demand the recall of the UN General Assembly, and urge our own government to support it.

28 September 2001

What is at stake now

We are now being told that we must give up some of our most important civil liberties as part of the price we have to pay to stop terrorism. The arguments used to justify this are easy to understand but, before we agree to change the law, we ought to think very carefully about the implications of what is proposed, and we might even ask ourselves exactly how tougher laws could have helped prevent Timothy McVeigh from blowing up that building in Oklahoma.

Terrorism is a political weapon, used by the weak against the strong, and historically it has never been defeated by repression but by negotiation, as when apartheid was replaced. Even in Northern Ireland, where the street violence and political hostility remain, it was not the Prevention of Terrorism Act which ended the bombing but the Good Friday Agreement, which started the talks about a political settlement. Even President Bush has been calling for Israeli–Palestinian talks to ease the tension and such talks will, soon, have to take place to establish and protect a Palestinian state.

The same is true with the underlying conflict of interests between the United States and the Arab world arising from the crude use of American military power to control the Middle East, which Washington believes is necessary to safeguard its global interests.

Britain, once an empire, was finally forced out of the Middle East when the Iranians nationalized their own oil industry, and later when Nasser defeated the Anglo-French forces which invaded Egypt in 1956. In neither case did anti-terrorism legislation play any part in solving these problems.

But repressive laws do serve another purpose, which suits the governments in America and Britain and many other countries as well: they offer a mechanism to control all dissidents, which they justify on the grounds that dissidents might be terrorists.

The introduction of identity cards, it is said, may be called 'Citizenship Rights Cards' – as if our rights are granted to us by the government, whereas in a democracy human rights are inherent and governments are granted their authority by the people, using their rights. We are also told that they will be smart cards, with electronic chips on them to make them harder to forge and easier to check – as if that will reassure us, when the truth is the exact opposite, for we will have no knowledge of what information is held on the card.

Anyone who has had any experience of dealing with the security services will know that they have records on over 300,000 people, and we must expect that this will be noted on our card, so that if the police stop you on the street they will know at once if you are a member of CND or read the *Morning Star*.

These cards could also include any information about previous arrests or convictions for even the most trifling offence: information, true or false, about your family, your home, your credit-rating and your car, with other details of your health-record, tax status and any suspicion about your entitlement to benefit – all this to be available to anyone entitled to check your card.

In South Africa the apartheid regime instituted the pass laws, which gave the police the right to detain anyone who did not carry their pass with them and provided the government with a complete system of control. This is why ANC activists burned their passes in an act of defiance.

I still have one wartime identity card which I have kept for 60 years, and it makes it clear that everyone has to carry their card at all times and produce it whenever required to do so by any civil or military authority, or be liable to be taken in for questioning. If, at that time, I forgot my card the police might well have smiled understandingly and said 'don't worry Mr Benn – just come round to the station in the next day or two if you have a moment' but it would be a different matter now for a homeless person, a peace campaigner, a trade unionist on strike, a Muslim with a beard who looked rather strange or an asylum-seeker.

Identity cards would be very welcome to every government in the world for their own reasons, but if they are introduced here we shall have lost our rights and they will not quickly be restored. We know this from all the emergency laws introduced in haste in wartime which still remain on the statute book.

There are also other dangers arising from this crisis and the economic problems which it has caused, with employers using these as an excuse to safeguard their profits by cutting pay or laying off workers. This could heighten social tensions and lead to a deterioration in race relations in our towns and cities.

This is a time when the labour and trade union move- ment and socialists here and internationally need to step up their efforts, not only to eliminate the manifest injustices which underlie some terrorism, but also to band themselves together to work for peace and democracy which are both under threat.

The anti-capitalist movement, born in Seattle, and very evident in Genoa, has wisely decided to refocus much of its efforts on the danger of war and the threat to civil liberties, including those to the ethnic communities and asylum-seekers. These are causes that all progressive people should join and support.

7 October 2001

This dangerous war

The warnings that are now being issued by President Bush and Tony Blair should be taken very seriously because they suggest that this war may be extended to any Muslim country that is suspected by Washington of harbouring terrorists, and it may continue for ten years.

This could mean that the Pentagon is already planning to renew the Gulf war with Iraq, that it wants to indicate to Iran that it too could be a target if it steps out of line. Moreover, it suggests that every pro-American government in the Middle East can rely on US military support if it is threatened by political movements that seem to be hostile.

Israel, which has enjoyed massive American support from the beginning, fears that its interests might be sacrificed to keep Arab governments in the coalition so hastily assembled, but Sharon has no intention of allowing a Palestinian state to be set up, and probably still has enough influence with President Bush to see it does not happen, when such a state is essential.

Despite all the claims that the bombing of Afghanistan has been authorized by the UN, the plain truth is that it has not, and the responsibility rests entirely with the United States and Britain who now claim, once again, to be the 'international community'. The decision to bring in NATO under Article 5, which makes an attack on one member an attack on all, is no substitute for UN approval, as NATO itself is committed, under its own constitution, to accept all the obligations provided for in the UN Charter.

The early arguments that those responsible for the atrocity against the World Trade Center must be brought to justice have been conveniently abandoned, as Osama bin Laden has already been convicted by name as the perpetrator, and ex-President Clinton announced, quite casually a few days ago, that he had personally authorized the assassination of bin Laden during his term as president. All this would make a fair trial impossible.

In any case, the United States will not cooperate with the world court because they have made it clear that no American, whatever he had done, would be extradited to face a prosecution in such a court, which ends the pretence that this whole operation is about justice in the sense that we understand it.

The oft-repeated argument that 'We have no quarrel with the people of Afghanistan' will not impress those innocent civilians who are now reeling under a succession of air-strikes that has already cut off their electricity supplies and thus knocked their water supplies and hospitals out of action.

And although Pakistan is being encouraged to take in desperate refugees from Afghanistan, now fleeing from their homes, you can be sure that neither Britain nor America have any plans to offer asylum to any of them, no doubt justifying that decision on the grounds that there might be terrorists among them. Nor should anyone be taken in by the gimmick of dropping humanitarian supplies of food and blankets from a great height, by parachute, to save the poor inhabitants of Afghanistan, millions of whom could well starve or freeze to death when the winter sets in in a few weeks' time

The principle that one nation can attack another nation which it believes may be harbouring terrorists is an open invitation to go back to the jungle and marks an end to the belief that international law should be respected.

This policy may well have implications for other Muslim states, the citizens of which, though totally opposed to terrorism, are not prepared to see the United States and its allies dictate the way the world is governed by threats to bomb and to invade whenever they think it is in their interests to do so. Mass protests have already occurred in Pakistan and as far away as Indonesia, and it is not impossible that the Saudi Arabian royal house might even be overthrown, which could threaten America's control of its huge oil supplies. This would almost certainly lead to direct US intervention to restore the king to his throne.

Despite the later denials that this war is a modern version of the Crusades, the use of that word by President Bush awakened the dangerous idea that we, the 'civilized Christian world', intend to teach the uncivilized Muslims who is in charge. In fact the war is not between civilized and uncivilized nations at all (if it were, the truly ancient civilizations in the Middle East could remind us of their much longer heritage and of the barbarity of Europe and America in our own imperial periods and during two world wars). This is a war for the control of raw materials dictated by the strategic interests of the United States, exactly as it was more than a hundred years ago when Britain dominated Egypt and the Gulf. Britain was thrown out of her empire, as America will be during this century.

Britain even invaded Afghanistan in August 1919 in a war to install a government that was more sympathetic to London, and we were defeated in 1842 when 15,000 British troops were massacred in the retreat from Kabul.

The Prime Minister would do better, at this moment, to be speaking for peace and the UN, rather than trailing along behind President Bush and encouraging him with policies that can only lead to disaster for us all.

12 October 2001

Truth in politics

'Truth', it is said, 'is the first casualty in war', and the events of the last few weeks have certainly proved this to be so, with the crude manipulation of the news by all governments reaching a point where it is very difficult to believe what is said by any government in any country, including this one.

The e-mail sent out by an adviser suggesting that the attack on the World Trade Center would provide an opportunity to slip out some bad news in the hope that it would not be noticed in the media is only one example of what is going on all the time, and someone I know from the inside told me that the only mistake made was to have put it in writing. However, compared with the really big issues on which we are being deliberately misled, this was a relatively insignificant example of what goes on all the time in the hope that we will accept what we are told uncritically.

The advertising industry was set up to sell goods to the public, but has now moved into the political world and is corrupting the democratic process to the point where it could even endanger its survival. Anyone in politics who wants to persuade people to listen has to do it effectively, whether in a speech or a broadcast, and there is nothing wrong with trying to assess public opinion, in advance, in order to understand the audience that will be listening.

Opinion polls are not now used to develop effective ways of getting an argument across but rather to determine the policy that should be followed – a technique perfected in focus groups where ideas are floated to test the reaction and not to assess the merits of the policies under consideration.

In short, the party bigwigs think they have found a way to control us by proxy, rather than allowing the democratic process to reach a conclusion. This is why the Labour conferences are so tightly managed and Labour MPs are expected to 'stay on message'. For once the line has been decided at the very top, everyone is expected to follow it, and there is a very sophisticated system run by the Labour headquarters to ensure that they do so.

As an MP I used to receive regular faxes from the Mill-bank Tower, with complete draft personalized press releases, containing 'quotations', supposedly from me, welcoming proposals coming from the government which I might never have heard of up to that point. I would be expected to pull it out of my fax and then fax it back to the local newspaper in my constituency, so they could run it as a story showing how united all Labour MPs were behind the government, as for example, 'Tony Benn welcomes compulsory homework for pensioners', and I once made a speech about this saying that I was beginning to feel more like an Avon lady than an MP. This had an amazing sequel, in that a few days later I received a furious letter from Avon bitterly complaining that I had dared to compare those hard-working women, doing doorstep selling, to MPs. Avon enclosed a box of cosmetics, the acceptance of which I feared might (in the case of an MP) constitute a corrupt practice – so I have been giving away deodorants and suntan lotion to all and sundry ever since.

This may all sound quite harmless, but it was an attempt to mislead the readers of the newspapers, and for that reason I never used any of these prefabricated press releases.

Now with the war against Afghanistan the government

campaign of mind-manipulation has gone much further, with daily briefings from the military about the success of the bombing and downplaying the claims of civilian casualties being caused. Moreover, the American and British governments have apparently been trying to prevent us from seeing the broadcasts by Osama bin Laden because they fear that they are having some impact on opinion in the West and cast doubt on the propaganda which reaches us every day from official sources in London and Washington.

When, during the Cold War, the Soviet Union jammed the BBC it was denounced by NATO, but during the Kosovo war NATO itself actually bombed the TV station in Belgrade to prevent it getting through to its own people. We are new hearing complaints about the Al-Jazeera Arab TV network (partly staffed by former members of the BBC Arabic Service before it was cut back) because it is attempting to let us hear the views of all sides.

During the Kosovo war we had a daily briefing from NATO headquarters on the progress of the operations some of which information later turned out to be inaccurate but it performed the function for which it was intended – to keep British public opinion behind the war. It is for the same reason that the hundreds of peace demonstrations around the world are reported so poorly – if at all; why our TV screens are full of aircraft and missiles complete with comments by military experts, and why speeches from MPs, when parliament was recalled, received so little coverage.

Today truth is more than a wartime casualty, it is permanently in intensive care, and that is why the *Morning Star* is absolutely essential, printing the news other papers do not publish, and giving its own opinions openly and without spin.

19 October 2001

History lessons and the future

The Prime Minister must be getting very worried about the latest opinion polls, which show that a clear majority of people here want a pause in the bombing of Afghanistan. His widely heralded, and much publicized, speech to the Welsh Assembly was carefully drafted and designed to swing the nation back towards support for more bombing, bombing for longer and to prepare us for a war that we are told could last for years.

He asked us to remember – as if we could ever forget – the human tragedy which engulfed those innocent people who died in New York on September 11 and the grief of their relatives who will mourn the loss of their loved ones for ever. But how can that justify the deaths of other equally innocent people who had nothing whatever to do with the attack on the World Trade Center, now living in the poorest country in the world and who are also dying and grieving for their own families in a war waged against them by the richest country in the world.

Reuben Schafer, an American who is 87 years old, and whose grandson Gregory actually died in the World Trade Center, attended a peace rally in New York, and read out a letter he had sent to President Bush, in which he wrote, 'Our government is using our son's memory as justification to cause suffering for other sons and parents in other lands.'

Last week Gerry Adams spoke in the Central Hall Westminster at a meeting to commemorate those who died in the hunger strike in Northern Ireland twenty years ago. This happened to take place on the very day that the prospects for peace were suddenly transformed by the most dramatic moves towards the demilitarization of the Six Counties, bringing peace out of terror. In the course of his speech Gerry Adams quoted Bobby Sands who wrote: 'Our revenge will be the laughter of our children' and those words said it all and offer us far more help for the future than demands for unthinking loyalty to fight a long war.

If we are serious about wanting peace we have got to eliminate the causes of war, and to do that we shall have to study our history a bit more carefully and not deliberately whip up more hatred which can only make things worse.

Nearly 22 years ago, in January 1980, the National Executive Committee of the Labour Party decided to send a delegation to see the then Soviet ambassador to protest against the Russian invasion of Afghanistan. I was asked to lead the delegation, with Eric Heffer and Joan Lestor.

Ambassador Lunkov received us, listened politely and then justified Moscow's decision to invade on the grounds that other countries, including Britain and America were arming exiles from Afghanistan to overturn the government in Kabul. He was, of course, referring to Osama bin Laden, then a hero in Washington, who was trained and funded by the CIA to be a freedom-fighter or terrorist (according to whose side you were on). Ironically, we are now preparing to invade the country to capture the same man for doing the same thing – only this time against his old masters. Such blatant hypocrisy completely undermines the credibility of the coalition case for what is being done now, and it needs to be exposed.

If we really want to see an end to terrorism and start building a new world order that will last, we shall have to adopt a completely different policy around the following principles:

1. An immediate end to the bombing of Afghanistan and a massive aid programme under the UN.
2. A return to the principles of the UN Charter, by which force can only be used by and with the consent of the Security Council and under its control.
3. The implementation of all UN resolutions on Israel (which the United States has vetoed 87 times), the immediate recognition of a Palestinian state and the closure of all the Jewish settlements.
4. The ending of all economic sanctions against Iraq (which have cost the lives of up to half a million children under five) and an end to the bombing of that country.
5. The withdrawal of all US troops from Saudi Arabia, sent there at the time of the Gulf War. (The presence of troops has caused great resentment in the Muslim world because of the significance of the Holy Places in Islam which are situated in that country.)
6. The establishment of an international court to try all those charged with war crimes, to which all countries including the United States and Britain would be subject, and a strict ban on assassination as an instrument of state policy.

7. A longer-term reform programme for the UN itself to make it more democratic: all delegates to the General Assembly to be elected in their countries of origin; and the UN to have the power to control the IMF, the WTO, the arms trade and the multinational corporations which now dominate the world.

A manifesto along these lines offers our best hope of uniting the global peace movement and laying the foundations for a durable understanding between the West and the Muslim world, without which our prospects of ending terrorism will remain remote.

This is what our government should be doing.

2 November 2001

Counting the cost

The advance of the Northern Alliance into Kabul marks a turning point in a continuing war waged by America and Britain, and this is the moment when the peace movement should reassess the situation in advance of Sunday's demonstration.

We shall no doubt be told that this is a famous victory, that it proves how successful the strategy has been and how wrong those who opposed the bombing were. The TV news bulletins have told us that women no longer have to wear the veil and will be allowed to go to school again – as if the whole operation had been planned with that in mind. There will be only passing references to the slaughter of Taliban soldiers who surrendered and few reminders of the appalling human rights record of the Northern Alliance when they were in power before, so as to prepare the way for them to go into a government of national unity headed by the king who has been elected by no one and has lived in exile for years.

To avoid taking on the responsibility for policing the new regime which would an impossible – and risky – task for US or British troops, the United Nations is to be allocated the task of clearing up the mess left by the air raids that have reduced Afghanistan to rubble and left enough cluster-bombs to kill or maim people for years ahead. All this has been achieved by high-level carpet-bombing by the United States that paved the way for the Northern Alliance to occupy Kabul, although they were asked to hold off.

We do not yet know whether the bombing of the south, which the Taliban still may control, will go on, but if it does the humanitarian crisis will worsen now that winter has come and little news has been allowed out recently about the situation facing the refugees.

Osama bin Laden has not yet been caught and even if he is, and is immediately assassinated, in line with the orders issued by President Bush, this is unlikely to weaken the Al-Qa'eda network and might even strengthen its appeal in the Muslim world.

Next we must be ready for a renewed war against Iraq which Richard Perle, former US Defense adviser, and still close to the present administration, has indicated is necessary, with all the consequences that might flow from that.

All that has been proved is that the mighty United States is militarily strong enough to bomb any nation in the world into submission and will no doubt be able to guarantee the building of the pipeline which it needs to get the Caspian oil to the market.

The UN has been reduced to the role of a relief agency, asked to pick up the pieces after a war but allowed to play no part in the development of policies that might have averted it. Moreover, Washington has successfully vetoed any suggestion that an international war crimes tribunal be set up, for fear that it might indict an American citizen.

This is imperialism writ large, with Britain tagging on to the tails of Uncle Sam, acting as its agent but with very little real influence. Our military input into the war has been insignificant; in addition to this we have lost any chance to use our position as a member of the UN Security Council, the European Council of Ministers or even the Commonwealth, where we could have played a more independent and positive part.

Another consequence of what has happened is that the Home Secretary is using this opportunity to introduce a state of emergency and impose imprisonment without trial on suspected persons. This is a flagrant contradiction of our claim that the war against terrorism was to protect our democratic rights and civilization.

This seems to me to be the situation as of today and it makes it all the more important that the peace movement should formulate clear demands that can be taken up world-wide and made the basis of an international campaign that will be needed if the crisis is not to get significantly worse in the months and years that lie ahead.

That is why the turnout on Sunday is so important, especially for the Muslim community in Britain, which feels itself to be under threat in the same way as the Irish community was a few years ago under the Prevention of Terrorism Act. This act was deliberately used as an instrument of repression, when in fact the answer to the situation lay in the talks that later took place and led to the Good Friday Agreement.

On Tuesday, the Islamic Centre in London held an important international conference to discuss the current situation. British and American imams, rabbis and Christian ministers met together for discussions that were entirely constructive and in marked contrast to the coverage of the war in the press and on TV.

Mick McGahey, the Scottish miners' leader, once said: 'It is not the weapons of war which frighten me but the desire of people to use them.' He pinpointed the terrible damage which the media have done over the last few weeks in whipping up hatred that will take literally years to overcome, leaving a legacy of intolerance and suspicion to poison the atmosphere for all of us in this country. And indeed this could well deteriorate if the economy slides into recession and those who are angry about unemployment start looking for scapegoats to blame.

16 November 2001

Preparing for war and working for peace

Within the next few months a new war may be launched by America against Iraq to remove Saddam Hussein by military force and install a puppet government taking orders from Washington to look after their interests and gain control of the oil in the region.

Our TV news bulletins will soon be full of pictures of US planes leaving the aircraft carriers and heading for Baghdad. Foreign correspondents in flak-jackets with video phones will be seen in front of burning buildings;

the official spokesmen in the White House will be reporting on the humanitarian nature of the operation; and intelligence briefings will be discreetly handed over to distinguished media commentators and broadcasters to 'help them with their articles and programmes'. We may even be told that the international community is supporting the war, when we all know that opposition world-wide is almost unanimous.

This is modern war as it is fought today by a superpower, and there are women now alive with their families in Baghdad who will be widows when the bombing starts and children who will be orphans. Those casualties will be dismissed as collateral damage and their deaths will be ignored, as have been the deaths of nearly half a million killed by the sanctions imposed on Iraq by the West.

The strategy behind all this was set out very clearly by the US Department of Defense and published on 30 May 2000 in a policy explanation. 'Full spectrum dominance' implies that US forces are able to conduct prompt, sustained and synchronized operations with combinations of forces tailored to specific situations and with access and freedom to operate in all domains – space, sea, land, air and information. 'Additionally, given the global nature of our interests and obligations, the United States must maintain its overseas forces' presence and the ability to rapidly project power world wide to achieve full spectrum dominance.'

In short, the United States has decided to tear up the UN Charter, scrap any international treaties it has signed, disregard the rule of law and set out to dominate the world. This is a threat to all of us and to peace itself.

What is being planned at this very moment in the

White House is a war of aggression and a threat to world peace, and we in Britain are expected to accept it and back the Americans on the grounds that we have a 'special relationship' with them and that if the British government dared to criticize them publicly the Prime Minister would lose all his influence with the President. In fact Mr Blair has virtually no influence in Washington at all. His real fear is that if he spoke out against the war President Bush could remove our nuclear weapons, discontinue the supply of warheads, cancel the technology links and switch off the global satellite system needed to target them, thus ending our pretence to be an independent nuclear power (which we are not).

Britain obviously does not have the power to stop the United States and neither does the EU, but we do have the power to demand that if the United States behaves unilaterally they cannot rely on retaining their bases here or any political support from us.

For all these reasons the peace movement in this country must be ready for our biggest campaign ever and it should have one specific objective: the withdrawal of all US bases from Britain and a flat rejection of any cooperation with the Star Wars project. This is the message which, coming through telegrams from American ambassadors all over the world back to the State Department in Washington, just might make them stop and think, because however strong you are, being hated across the globe (as they would be) would be a threat to their interests.

The Bush policy of revenge bombing has been tried by Sharon against the Palestinians, and has failed. A growing number of Israelis, including many ex-officers, are now demanding a real solution that recognizes a Palestinian state and involves withdrawal from the occupied territories. This offers the only real hope of a lasting peace.

We should, however, occasionally, remind ourselves of the other America and what it stood for, as set out in a historic statement recently republished:

> The way chosen by the United States was plainly marked by a few clear precepts . . . All humanity shares a common hunger for peace and fellowship and justice . . . No nation's security can be lastingly achieved in isolation, but only in effective cooperation with fellow nations . . . Any nation's attempt to dictate other nations their form of government is indefensible . . . A nation's hope of lasting peace cannot be firmly based upon any race in armaments but rather upon just relations and honest understanding with all other nations . . . faithful to the spirit that inspired the United Nations . . . to control and to reduce armaments . . . to allow all nations to devote their energies to the tasks of healing the war's wounds, of clothing and feeding and housing the needy, of perfecting a just political life, of enjoying the fruits of their own free toil.

These are not the words of some young left-wing idealist, but of General Dwight D. Eisenhower, a Republican president who was in the White House nearly 50 years ago, and who knew from experience what war meant.

The American peace movement now wants to link up with others world-wide, and Eisenhower has given a lead we can follow.

22 February 2002

War is a moral issue

Parliament has now adjourned until October, and with it has gone the possibility of MPs holding the government to account for what it is doing, leaving it free to plan a war against Iraq which may start at any time. The Prime Minister has said that no decision has yet been taken, but every time President Bush speaks he reaffirms his determination to launch that war and he expects Britain to give its support. The exact date on which the bombing will begin may not have been decided in Washington, but detailed military cooperation between the Pentagon and the Ministry of Defence must be taking place on a daily basis.

It is reported that the first stage will be a massive series of air attacks to be followed by an invasion involving over 200,000 US troops. Apparently British forces numbering over 20,000 may be added, but it is the political support from London and not the military contribution from this country that the Americans really need.

This war will be in defiance of the UN Charter, which only authorizes the use of military force when it has been decided by the Security Council with the support of the five permanent members including France, Russia and China. If Britain joins in we will be guilty of conducting an act of aggression and committing war crimes against those innocent civilians who are bound to be killed.

For there are many women now living in Baghdad who will be widows within a few months, children who will be orphans and homeless as result of actions by British airmen or soldiers acting in our name. The responsibility for this will lie with the Prime Minister personally, who will have taken this decision without the authority of a vote in the House of Commons.

The new Archbishop of Canterbury, Dr Rowan Williams, appointed this week, has made it absolutely clear that he will not support this war unless the UN has given its authority. (This comes from a man who has actually taken direct action in the anti-nuclear campaigns in the past.)

I do not know whether the Prime Minister appreciates the enormity of the choice that he would be making to defy the UN, break international law and kill people at the behest of President Bush. If in the event he does take that view, he could well forfeit his claim to the support of all those across the whole spectrum of British opinion who see war as a moral issue. He will also destroy his own moral authority and relieve us of any obligations we may have to respect him.

For so long as he can maintain his majority in parliament he will, in law, be able to retain his office and his power, but from that moment he will have lost his right to be believed or trusted, and the only people who can save him from making such a disastrous mistake are other Labour MPs, whether the House is in recess or not. This is why, over these summer months, a massive public campaign is required to alert all ministers and MPs to their duty and to warn them of their own responsibility to those who elected them.

I know that many Conservatives and Liberal Democrats are opposed to the war, but they must act quickly because, if and when the war begins, the government will try to shield behind the men and women that they have sent into battle by telling us that we must support our own troops.

Quite apart from the moral arguments against this war, the consequences in the Middle East and elsewhere, if it takes place, would inflame the whole region. This could well lead to the toppling of some regimes that have been obedient to America but whose populations deeply resent the impact of American imperialism on their lives.

You can be sure that Sharon and the Israeli government are pushing as hard as they can for this attack on Iraq to begin, because it could remove the one country that might be able to protect the Palestinians and would justify their own brutal repression in the West Bank and Gaza.

What is needed now is an initiative by some of the most senior statesmen in the world to alert humanity to the danger that faces us. If people of the stature of Nelson Mandela, Mikhail Gorbachev, Ted Heath, Jimmy Carter, Mary Robinson, Ahmed ben Bella, Boutros Boutros-Ghali and others issued a strong statement reaffirming their commitment to the UN Charter, then this tragedy might be averted.

The rest of us must be free to respond as we think best, recalling that our task must be to persuade and not frighten people as a result of what we do. At present, fear is being used as a cruel means to drive us into war, and the military–industrial complex in America will no doubt be arguing that the best answer to the stock market crash and risk of a slump is a huge rearmament programme and a war.

I hope that those who advise the Prime Minister are alerting him to the danger confronting him personally if he gets this wrong. In 1956 Sir Anthony Eden, the then prime minister, launched an attack against Egypt, comparing President Nasser to Hitler. He was subsequently forced to resign in disgrace, and was succeeded by Harold Macmillan, the Chancellor of the Exchequer.

A war with Iraq, which would certainly alienate Russia and China, and many of our European partners as well, could cost Tony Blair his job, undermine public support for the government as a whole and inflict untold suffering on millions of people. It must be prevented.

26 July 2002

Expect war – prepare for peace

On Monday, as we commemorate the first anniversary of the attack on the World Trade Center, we must try to understand the political consequences and face the new dangers posed by the determination of Bush and Blair to launch a new Middle Eastern War.

No country, however powerful, can escape the risk of a terrorist attack, showing the Star Wars project to be useless, but the suffering of the people of Vietnam, Afghanistan and Iraq should remind us that a superpower, with its massive armoury of weapons, can inflict greater damage.

It is the elimination of violence in international relations that should concern us most, and that requires us to concentrate upon the need for justice and a revitalized UN.

No one can possibly accept the arguments now coming from the White House that if the United States decides that any other country is hostile and has acquired modern weapons, America is entitled to make pre-emptive military attacks. If we did so, the world would have accepted jungle law based upon revenge and naked aggression, while soldiers would be permanently exempted from any risk of prosecution in an international criminal court.

The threat to our freedom does not necessarily come

from enemies abroad. In recent months freedom in both Britain and America has been gravely undermined by the draconian measures taken allegedly to safeguard civil liberties, and this has taken place without a shot being fired. One of the most vivid examples of this was provided on Tuesday, when the Prime Minister summoned a press conference in Sedgefield for journalists who represent no one but the media bosses for whom they work, while MPs elected to look after servicemen and women, who may be called to sacrifice their lives in the war, were denied the right to meet and decide policy.

The closing down of parliament when all the important discussions about Iraq are going on privately in Washington and London reveals the arrogance of executive power in its attitude to those who have the responsibility for questioning ministers and holding them to account. In doing this, New Labour can rely upon the backing of the Tory leader who has himself demanded full support for the war that Bush wants, thus creating, in effect, a coalition government and a war Cabinet that seeks to obliterate all serious debate.

Yet despite this, the peace movement in Britain is stronger than ever. All the opinion polls suggest that there are clear majorities against the war, both inside the trade union movement, inside the Labour Party (including Sedgefield) in parliament and nationally. The credit for this belongs to all those who, despite the systematic failure to report them and the vilification to which they have been subjected, have argued their case and organized STOP THE WAR meetings all over the country, leading to the great demonstration on 28 September in London.

Of the many who deserve credit for alerting the public

to the dangers of war have been Tam Dalyell, the Father of the House of Commons, his fellow parliamentarians Alice Mahon, George Galloway, Alan Simpson, Jeremy Corbyn and those in the Labour, Communist, Socialist Worker and Green parties who, along with progressive trade union leaders and campaigning journalists such as Paul Foot, John Pilger, Tariq Ali and Robert Fisk have succeeded in breaking through the establishment censorship.

World-wide opinion is also hardening against war. This opposition is led by a diverse group of well-known figures who, for very different reasons, have spoken out, against military action. They include Kofi Annan, Nelson Mandela, Henry Kissinger and many leaders in the Arab world and Europe. In America itself resistance to the war is also growing, with barely half the population now favouring an attack on Iraq and Congressional leaders increasingly demanding the right to vote before the President launches the attack he is planning.

But after the statements made by Bush and Blair we must be ready for that war to be launched within the next few months. We must be clear also about how we should respond when the bombs drop on Baghdad and the casualty figures mount, including, very probably, those of British soldiers.

The consequences in the Middle East could be catastrophic, leading to the toppling of the Saudi government, an interruption of oil supplies and escalating oil prices that will adversely affect the world economy. There may also be an extension of the Israeli war against the Palestinians to include Iraq, possibly even involving a nuclear threat by Israel which has weapons of mass destruction and is ready to use them.

In addition to the campaign to stop the war we should now be demanding that a Middle East peace conference be convened at once, under the auspices of the UN. This would secure the acceptance by Iraq of weapons inspectors, combined with the immediate ending of sanctions and the bombing to enforce the no-fly zones. It would also bring about the establishment and recognition of a Palestinian state within the frontiers set out by the UN, the immediate withdrawal of the Israeli army and the resettlement of the Arab refugees backed by massive aid programmes.

Nothing less than that, combined with a renewed effort to secure global disarmament, can avert the dangers which now confront humanity and give us a chance to build a fairer and more peaceful world.

6 September 2002

An alternative dossier on the Iraq crisis

Next Tuesday, the House of Commons will be presented with a dossier designed to persuade MPs that the weapons of mass destruction possessed by Saddam Hussein justify a war to overthrow him. This dossier may only be released hours before the debate begins, which will make it impossible for MPs to study it or assess its credibility. The Prime Minister has apparently refused to allow a vote, in an attempt to silence the opposition and create the false impression that he enjoys full support.

The following facts are offered as an alternative dossier:

- On 19–20 December 1983 Donald Rumsfeld met Saddam Hussein in Baghdad, and later told the *New York Times* that 'it struck us as useful to have a relationship, given that we were interested in solving the Mideast problems'.

- On 1 January 1984 the *Washington Post* reported that the United States, 'in a shift in policy, has informed friendly Persian Gulf nations that the defeat of Iraq in the 3-year-old war would be "contrary to US interests"'.

- On 24 March 1984 Donald Rumsfeld returned to Baghdad for talks with Tariq Aziz just after the UN released its report, later confirmed by the US State Department which issued a statement saying that 'available evidence indicates that Iraq has used lethal chemical weapons'.

- On 29 March 1984 the *New York Times* reported from Baghdad that 'American diplomats pronounced themselves satisfied with relations between Iraq and the United States'.

- Throughout the period when Rumsfeld was President Reagan's Middle East envoy, the White House was authorizing the purchase by Iraq of American equipment including helicopters, and US intelligence sources told the *Los Angeles Times* in 1991 that they 'believe that the American-built helicopters were among those dropping the poisonous gas'.

- The Senate Committee on US Chemical and Biological Warfare-related Dual Use Exports to Iraq, dated 25 May and 7 October 1994, reported that from 1985, if not earlier, until 1989, a veritable witch's brew of biological weapons was exported to Iraq by private American suppliers pursuant to application and licensing by the US Department of Commerce.

- Among the chemical materials exported were *Bacillus anthracis*, *Clostridium botulinum*, *Histoplasma capsulatum*, *Brucella melitensis*, and *Escherichia coli*, all deadly biological weapons and identical to those found and removed by the UN inspectors sent in on behalf of the UN after the Gulf War.

All these facts have been published in the United States, and if the Government of Iraq were to publish its own account of American weapons supplies and political support we would have a much better understanding of what went on and why.

In addition to these facts MPs should recall the following:

- Israel is also in breach of UN resolutions. It has an even bigger arsenal, including nuclear weapons of mass destruction, has invaded the Lebanon, bombed Iraq and denies the Palestinians their rights. No one, quite rightly, wants a war against Sharon, which the peace movement would oppose with all its strength.
- The United States has bombed the following countries since 1945: China, Korea, Guatemala, Indonesia, Cuba, Congo, Peru, Laos, Vietnam (where a million people died), Cambodia, Grenada, Libya, El Salvador, Nicaragua, Panama, Iraq, Sudan, Afghanistan, and Yugoslavia.
- President Reagan denounced the USSR as an evil empire threatening the West. He persecuted the peace movement and we now know that no such plan to attack NATO ever existed in Moscow.
- The US Department of Defense published a policy statement on 30 May 2000 setting the goal of achieving a 'combination of forces tailored to specific situations

and with access to and freedom to operate in all domains – space, sea, land, air and information . . . and the ability to rapidly project power world-wide in to achieve full spectrum dominance'.

- During the Suez crisis Nasser was compared to Hitler and those who opposed the war were denounced as appeasers.
- The UN Charter is committed to the peaceful settlement of disputes. It makes no provision for one country to attack another in order to change the regime.
- President Bush in his speech to the General Assembly delivered an ultimatum to the UN as well as to Saddam Hussein, and that too was a threat to peace.

It would be a total corruption of the whole meaning and spirit of the UN Charter, which was carefully written to make possible the peaceful settlement of international disputes, to try to present it as offering a blank cheque for war whenever the United States wants one.

It is the double standards, the hypocrisy, the threat to innocent lives, the propaganda, the brutality, the waste and the suffering of war, and its aftermath, that motivates the peace movement and which has to be expressed and articulated, as it will be at the national demonstration on 28 September.

20 September 2002

Questions that must be answered

Last weekend it was made clear in Washington that if the UN Security Council did not pass the resolution put forward by the American government that would authorize a war against Iraq, the United States would find no difficulty in assembling an international coalition to join them in that war.

Given the total and uncritical support given to President Bush's war plans by the Prime Minister, it must be obvious that Britain would be the key player in that coalition. This is not so much because our armed forces are needed, but rather because our political support is essential. For even in America many people would oppose a war if the UN did not approve it and if Britain stood aside. That is why Blair's war mission to Moscow and around the world has been so important to Bush.

It is not yet clear when the war will begin – that will depend on the Congressional elections, the weather and the speed with which US forces can be assembled. However, from the moment Bush says he will act alone, and Blair formally indicates his support, a number of questions arise which the government must answer because of their importance to our own people:

- Will Britain be, in a legal sense, in a state of war with Iraq if we join the US attack?
- Why did President Bush have to get a vote in Congress authorizing the use of force, when the British government has not indicated its intention of doing so?
- If British forces are engaged, will it be done under the royal prerogative, which requires no parliamentary authority?
- What will be the position of British citizens now living and working in Iraq: will they be advised to leave

the country before the attack, or to stay, and if the latter, what protection can the government give to them?

- Will British troops, if captured, be entitled to be treated in accordance with the Geneva Convention?

- Will British troops be under the orders of American officers, and will they be required to serve in an army of occupation?

- Will the British government be consulted as to the date when hostilities begin? Will it be a signatory of any agreement to bring the war to an end?

- What compensation will the British government give to those British citizens who suffer a financial loss as a result of the War?

- Will Iraqi citizens living in Britain be treated as enemy aliens and imprisoned, and under what statutory authority?

- What rights will Iraqi soldiers captured by British forces have? Will they qualify for the protection of the Geneva Convention?

- What will be the position, under military law, of members of the British armed forces who refuse to fight because they believe that a war waged against Iraq that has not been authorized by the UN could lead to their being charged at a war crimes tribunal under the International Criminal Court, which the British government supports?

- How would the position of British troops charged with war crimes differ from the position of American troops, given that the United States has declared itself exempt from any International Criminal Court?

- How would the British government respond to a charge of war crimes, of a kind brought under the Nuremberg trials?
- Have the law officers been consulted on these issues and will their report be published and laid before parliament?

These are just a few of the unanswered questions arising from the situation now facing the British parliament and people. They must be answered because they affect the lives and property of hundreds of thousands of British citizens who could be caught up in this war, as well as those Iraqis who may die.

If we do go to war and the government fails to provide satisfactory answers and safeguards, the full responsibility will rest upon the Prime Minister personally, who, if he uses the royal prerogative, will be the one man taking all the decisions. It is thus not impossible that he could face charges of war crimes or crimes against humanity. These would have been committed in our name, using taxes we have paid, without the authority of the parliament we elect or the Security Council set up under the UN Charter to which Britain is committed by solemn international undertakings.

These are questions that we should all be discussing and raising with all MPs, because they have an opportunity to press them in the Commons and secure answers, and if they fail to do so they will share the moral responsibility for what happens.

1 November 2002

5

Foreign Affairs and Defence

What sort of Europe?

The debate about the future of Europe has been reawakened by Gerhard Schröder, the German Chancellor, who is supporting a plan that would absorb all the nations in the EU into a federal superstate with its own central government.

This plan, based on the German model which unites and controls their states (or *Länder*) would convert the parliaments of Britain and the other member countries into a mixture of regional assemblies and glorified local authorities all subject to the authority of the centre. In this superstate the real power would be in the hands of the president of the Commission, who is appointed and not elected, and he would then have the right to appoint the other, unelected, commissioners to form his Cabinet.

The prime ministers from the separate nations would be bundled together in a second chamber, as a part of the European parliament, with no executive authority over the countries which elected them. The whole concept is political rather than economic. It is the boldest plan yet produced by a European leader and its implications need to be publicly debated during the general election, so that we can get clear answers from all our political leaders and candidates before we vote.

New Labour hoped that Europe and the euro could be kept out of the election campaign because the Millbank Tower pollsters know very well that the public is strongly opposed to the sacrifices of our independence, and the Tories might well win votes by presenting themselves as the sole defenders of our autonomy and of the pound sterling. This is why the government has cooked up five economic tests that have to be fulfilled before Britain can join the euro, as if some Treasury computer could tell us when to give up the democratic control of our own economy.

The integration of Europe is a political and not an economic question. It must be seen as such, since each step taken in that direction shifts power from the elected to the unelected, and this raises fundamental democratic questions.

It is very important that those on the Left who oppose this do so because it represents a steady erosion of the power of the electors who are not taken in by the crude nationalism of the Right, with their dislike of foreigners and strange commitment to the Queen's image on bank-notes. What are the alternatives for those of us who are socialists, democrats and internationalists who do want to cooperate closely with European neighbours?

In theory it would be possible to have a genuinely democratic United States of Europe, along the lines of the American model, with an elected president, Senate and House of Representatives all accountable to the people. But to do so would involve the complete abolition of the Commission, the Council of Ministers and the Central Bank in Frankfurt. For these reasons it would be totally acceptable to the European establishment because it would reveal their deep dislike of democracy, and would in practice be both unwieldy and unworkable.

What the Left in Europe should be working for is a Commonwealth that brings in all the nations, east and west, committed to cooperate with each other and harmonize their policies, step by step, with the consent of each of their parliaments, rather like a mini UN, with an Assembly and Council of Ministers to oversee it, but with no power to impose on those countries that want to pursue policies that meet their own particular circumstances. This would need to be underpinned by the closest links between the trade unions and other progressive popular organizations across the whole continent.

What we do not want is to go back to the old hostility between the individual countries which led to two world wars – and that is the danger of following the Tory Party line.

Internationalism is the proper response to globalization, and those who believe that a federal Europe would protect us from the power of the multinational corporations are completely wrong, for the European Commission is little more that a regional agent of globalization, enforcing the diktats of the bankers in our own continent.

We are told that soon after the election we shall have the referendum on the euro, and in some ways it will be a more important choice than the one we have to make on 7 June, for if Britain is persuaded to join the single currency we shall, forever, have lost the right of self-government through the ballot box and all key decisions will be taken by those we did not elect and cannot remove.

In the days ahead, before polling day comes, we should raise all these questions at public meetings and in our questions to the candidates, to be sure that our democracy is not taken from us.

4 May 2001

Real politics begins on 8 June

Last weekend, I spoke at four May Day rallies, including those at Edinburgh, Glasgow and Chesterfield, all packed with people, many of them young and all of them really committed to socialism and the Labour movement. It was inspiring and exciting, and it turned my mind to 8 June – the day after the election. For whatever divisions there may be now, as between different candidates on the Left, we know that after the polling stations have closed, a new alliance has to be forged to campaign for the things that need to be done.

The biggest and most important of these is the campaign to stop a new arms race which President Bush intends to launch with his nuclear missile defence project, or 'Son of Star Wars'. That project has very little to do with defending the world's greatest superpower from a crippling nuclear assault launched from Libya, Iraq or North Korea which, we are told, now pose a deadly threat to peace. Admiral Eugene Carroll, a very distinguished American naval officer who has held high command in the past, came to the House of Commons recently to explain that NMD was a project designed to establish a total military command of the planet by the United States. He pointed out that, if it works – which is by no means certain – it would allow American space stations to destroy any land installation on the globe by laser-beams. He called on us to organize what he called 'more Greenham Commons' to see that Britain is not sucked into this scheme by making Fylingdales and Menwith Hill available.

No doubt, with the American economy in recession, the military–industrial complex, which President Eisenhower warned us against in his farewell address, went to see President Bush to tell him that a big arms programme could put the American economy back on course. Having funded the Republicans last year, the military–industrial interest is now expecting a pay-off from the man they put in the White House.

The Prime Minister, the Foreign Secretary and Alastair Campbell have been trying to persuade us that this is a sensitive matter that has to be handled sensitively in order to keep the Star Wars issue off the agenda until the election is over. But there is no doubt whatever that when the present administration has been re-elected they will give their full support to this act of madness, despite the widespread opposition across the whole spectrum of Labour opinion, as well as in Europe, Russia and China.

The reason is that the so-called 'special relationship', which is supposed to unite Washington and London, is a semi-colonial relationship based on the fact that America supplies us with nuclear weapons and allows us to pretend that we have an independent deterrent. In return, the United States controls our intelligence services and dictates our foreign and defence policies, and also provides our Trident submarines with a communications system without which the warheads cannot be targeted.

As minister responsible for nuclear energy during many years in the Cabinet, I actually had to go to Washington to appear before Dr Glenn Seaborg, the Chairman of the United States Atomic Energy Commission, to get their permission to develop our own nuclear policy. Moreover, the security officer in my department told me that his job was to persuade the United States that their intelligence supervision was satisfactory.

Thus, if Britain were to say no to Star Wars, the United States could withdraw our warheads and we would be seen as a second-class power in nuclear terms, with all the domestic political consequences that would follow. That is why the Opposition has come out so strongly in favour of Star Wars, and why their demands for a clear statement in support of Star Wars have caused such embarrassment to the Prime Minister.

All this will become clear once the election is out of the way and the Campaign for Nuclear Disarmament, Labour Action for Peace and all the other peace organizations in Britain will need to get together quickly to plan a campaign to stop support for Star Wars.

These matters should be raised during the election, but we know that our real work begins on 8 June and we need to be thinking now about how to build a winning coalition to see it does not happen.

I am very optimistic about the future because with another Labour Government safely installed for a second term some of the restraints which have held the party back during this first term for 'New Labour' will be lifted and we shall be free once more to work openly and

co-operatively for peace, trade union rights, environmental protection and pensions linked to earnings in a
way that really cannot be frustrated any longer.

'New Labour' has passed its sell-by date. The Labour
movement will come into its own and I hope reunite
socialists in a way that will surprise the focus groups and
the spin-doctors who are so keen on soundbites and
commercial marketing that they have forgotten why the
Labour movement was set up and why it has to work
internationally for peace and social justice.

11 May 2001

War crimes and justice

In the world of today some new international system of
justice to try and punish those guilty of crimes against
humanity is clearly necessary to limit the excesses of brutality which are so common. But if such a court is to be
respected and effective it must be established by the UN
and be authorized to examine all complaints against all
nations. Moreover, every member-state must submit itself
to the jurisdiction of that court and be ready to extradite
its own citizens for trial under its provisions.

We cannot accept the double standards which now
exist which allow suspected war criminals in some countries to be protected by one superpower. The United
States itself has made it clear that it will never allow one
of its own citizens to be arraigned and tried, however
serious the crime that person may have committed.

Each nation that did accept the jurisdiction of such a
world court would also have to agree to follow its own

constitutional procedures before an extradition took place. By these simple criteria the extradition of Slobodan Milosevic to The Hague could not be justified. The court dealing with offences committed in former Yugoslavia could not try a US president who had ordered the killing of civilians by bombing with depleted uranium in a war that was launched in breach of the UN Charter and ignored many other crimes committed elsewhere in the world. For instance, what about the Israeli policy of ethnically cleansing Palestinians and invading southern Lebanon? Or Turkish planes that bomb the Kurds in northern Iraq? Or the sanctions that have killed hundreds of thousands of innocent Iraqis?

In writing this I am not endorsing the things done by Milosevic, but if you believe, as I do, that all modern warfare is a crime which does not differentiate between the innocent and the guilty, then his actions in protecting his country from NATO attacks may be seen in a different light.

The Serbs, who are now so systematically demonized by world leaders and the media, were for centuries occupied by the Turks, then by the Austro-Hungarian Empire and then, most recently, in the Second World War, were slaughtered in their hundreds of thousands by the Croatian fascists who were allied to Hitler.

Indeed, before the Russians entered the war in 1941 and before Pearl Harbor brought in the Americans, Serbia declared war on Nazi Germany and were our staunchest ally. Their leader, Marshal Tito, was armed and highly praised by Churchill. Later, when Tito broke with Stalin, he was hailed as a hero in the West, armed and received on a state visit to London. His economic reforms, drawing upon the ideas of industrial democracy, were regarded as positive.

But as Germany revived and became strong it began to work out how it could reassert its control of the Danube, and to do this it had to secure the destruction of the Yugoslav federation.

Croatia was recognized – and John Major went along with this reluctantly – having been promised an opt-out for Britain from the EU Social Chapter. Genscher, the then German Foreign Minister, declared that the break-up of Yugoslavia had been his greatest achievement.

The Bosnian war followed and then, two years ago, NATO attacked in force, on the grounds that it was defending the rights of the Albanians in Kosovo, who under the leadership of the Kosovo Liberation Army were engaged in open warfare and were armed by Germany and America.

The war came after Milosevic had rejected an ultimatum which demanded that he allow NATO to station forces all over his country, which no one could accept. Some people believe that the eviction of the Kosovan Albanians began in earnest because Belgrade saw them as NATO allies in that war.

Now Macedonia is going through the same process, with the West doing little to help the government there resist this next Albanian onslaught. As the crisis deepens, the United States and Germany are rubbing their hands at the thought that they now control the Balkans and this will permit the safe passage of the oil from the Near East.

The extradition of Milosevic was secured, against the judgment of the Constitutional Court in Belgrade, by a crude bribe offered to the new tame Serbian government of well over a billion dollars to rebuild the economy, which NATO was busy destroying only two years earlier.

And you can be sure that the profits from the NATO war will have gone into the pockets of the US arms manufacturers, and the profits from rebuilding the infrastructure will also go into the pockets of some major US construction firms.

None of this exonerates Milosevic from the crimes he has committed, but neither does it take us an inch nearer the day when other well-known war criminals who enjoy Western support – and far closer to home – may be tried for what they have done over the years.

It was often the practice, in the past, for the victors to capture the leaders they had defeated and execute them, but that sort of revenge has nothing whatever to do with justice and the purchase of Milosevic with Western dollars is no basis for a world system of law we can respect.

6 July 2001

Trident: a moral issue

On Wednesday, in the Conway Hall in London, Angie Zelter of the Trident Ploughshares Group launched her new book, *Trident on Trial*,[1] in which she writes about the work to which she has devoted herself, namely to draw attention to the danger to humanity posed by nuclear weapons.

She quotes the obligations which Britain undertook

[1] Angie Zeller, *Trident on Trial* (Trident Ploughshares, 2001 www.tridentploughshares.org).

when it signed the Non Proliferation Treaty (NPT), 'to negotiate in good faith a nuclear disarmament', reinforced by its signature of the statement issued in 2000, when the NPT was reviewed, containing 'an unequivocal undertaking by the nuclear weapons states to accomplish the total elimination of nuclear arsenals'.

When it became clear to her, and others, that the government has no intention whatsoever of doing anything to fulfil these obligations and is actually upgrading its nuclear arsenal, and is likely to support the US Star Wars project, they decided to take direct non-violent action to dismantle our war machine.

Angie has now been arrested over a hundred times and has served no less than sixteen prison sentences, which is a testament to her commitment. In her court appearances she has been able to make use of the advisory opinion of the International Court of Justice which ruled that 'the threat or use of nuclear weapons would generally be contrary to the rules of international law . . . and states must never use weapons that are incapable of distinguishing between civilian targets'.

In one case Angie and her colleagues were actually acquitted in the Sheriff's Court in Greenock after this evidence had been submitted as part of the defence, although the government has chosen to disregard it.

Britain has spent over twelve billion pounds on the Trident nuclear programme, and it costs about a million pounds a year to maintain and upgrade it. Trident carries 48 100-kiloton warheads, far more powerful than the atom bomb dropped on Hiroshima which killed almost 150,000 people, devastated the city, destroying 18 hospitals, 14 high schools and 13 Christian churches.

Having visited Hiroshima and Nagasaki and met some of the survivors, it is impossible not to see that attack as a war crime and act of genocide because there was no distinction made between the military and civilian targets.

One of the most moving exhibits in the Hiroshima exhibition is of a schoolchild's metal lunch-box which had been literally melted into a shapeless blob next to a faint mark on the stone steps, outside the school, where the child itself had been sitting when it was burned alive by the heat.

Angie, and those who work with her in Trident Plough-shares, including Ulla Roder and Ellen Moxley, are heroines of the highest order because they have accepted a moral responsibility to do what they can by direct action to prevent a nuclear war.

If they were working in China they would have been awarded the Nobel Peace prize, but here they are marginalized and ignored by the mass media, unless a scuffle at Faslane can provide a good newspaper photo. Interestingly, some well-known Labour MPs who were once active in CND now support our nuclear programme and denounce those who still oppose it.

When the history of the peace movement comes to be written it is those who have taken a stand and suffered for it who will be remembered as the real prophets of our time. They deserve all the support that they can get, for the importance of those who are witnesses for peace goes far beyond the issue that they take up, in that they remind us that in the end we are accountable to our own consciences for the lives we lead and the things we do.

Having been brought up on Bible stories which were about the conflict between the kings who had power and the prophets who preached righteousness, I can understand why the Moderator of the Church of Scotland, the Archbishop of Wales[1] and the leader of the Iona Community have decided to give their own support to the Trident Ploughshares movement.

Trident on Trial should be compulsory reading for all those who care about the survival of the human race and what the courage of individuals can do to uphold the sanctity of human life against those world leaders who are always engaged in some highly publicized 'peace process' here and everywhere, while secretly preparing even more deadly weapons of war.

Not many of us have the strength of character or sense of personal commitment to do what Angie and her fellow peacemakers are doing, but we can and should give them all the support and encouragement we are able to.

And if we do so we can build a strong body of public opinion that can develop into a political movement that no government can disregard. We know this from the indications already available from Scotland which show that 51 per cent of the population are behind those who engaged in the sit-down at Faslane and 58 per cent are against spending public money on Trident.

Unless we can stop them, the deadly patrols of Trident will go on with one of them at sea 24 hours a day, seven days a week, carrying warheads capable of mass destruction. Each of them will be doing so by default, with our implied authority and support.

13 July 2001

---

[1] Dr Rowan Williams, now Archbishop of Canterbury.

Leaving the American Empire

Throughout the whole of human history many empires have grown, dominated and finally withered away. We now live at a time when the American Empire is at its peak. The United States has bases all over the world. Four new ones have just been added in Pakistan, Afghanistan, Uzbekistan and Tajikistan, which offer control of the oil in the Caspian Sea.

The Pentagon war machine can, by high-level bombing, flatten and destroy any land installations almost anywhere and without the loss of life associated with past empires. Thus the American's can enforce their will on any government for any purpose they choose.

The Star Wars project, when it comes into operation, will allow any American president to order the destruction of any installation in the world from space stations using laser-beams, without the necessity of deploying any troops at all. To do this all international treaties that might obstruct these plans must be abandoned, as we have seen with the unilateral ditching by America of the Anti Ballistic Missile Treaty which might have restricted the project.

New legislation is now being introduced into Congress called the 'American Servicemembers Protection Act', which would give the President the authority to send US forces to snatch back any American military personnel who might be arraigned before an International War Crimes Tribunal, and would penalize any developing countries that voted for such a court to be set up. This follows the enactment of the Patriot Act which already allows any non-US citizen suspected of being associated with terrorism to be tried before a military tribunal which would have the power to withhold the evidence from the accused and his or her lawyers, and impose the death-sentence on the vote of a bare majority of the officers making up the tribunal.

All these fly in the face of all the human rights developments upheld by the UN. Indeed, it all amounts to the tearing up of the Charter itself, since nobody, but nobody, is to be allowed to limit the infinite power required by the new empire based in Washington.

Against this background any pretence that Britain, Europe, or even Russia or China, can have any real influence on America is a complete illusion. It would be better if we were told the truth, namely that America has no intention of being told what to do by world opinion or even the so-called international community, which is the new instrument for world governance.

None of this is really new, for the Romans did the same during the 500 years when they controlled Europe, as did the Arabs when their crescent-shaped dominion stretched from the Indus to Spain.

Genghis Khan and the Mogul emperors also retained full control after their conquests, as did Britain, France, Portugal and Spain in their respective empires built up during the sixteenth to the nineteenth centuries. Later, in the twentieth century, Hitler, Mussolini and Emperor Hirohito of Japan proclaimed their power before and during the Second World War.

Britain is now entirely in the power of Washington. With US bases here, an 'independent deterrent' in the form of Trident submarines equipped with atomic warheads, which the Americans only lend us, and with the

United States controlling the global satellite guidance system we would need to target our weapons, our negotiating position is so weak as to be virtually non-existent.

However, that has not prevented the Prime Minister parading around the world as if he were the vice-president and speaking of the war as if Britain was playing a significant role – which is not the case – but all this should not take us in, nor could it if we sit and think about the underlying truth.

We simply cannot force the Americans to do anything we want, or even to respect international law, but that does not leave us as powerless as might appear to be the case. The time has come when we should be discussing a different strategy: namely a plan for withdrawal from our close links with the United States into a more non-aligned position.

This would mean first the abandonment of the pretence that we are a nuclear power and asking America to withdraw their military bases from this country. We know from experience that they would reject the request, just as they did when the Cuban government asked the Americans to leave the Guantanamo Bay base in their country. However, a non-nuclear, non-aligned Britain could throw its full weight behind the UN and its various agencies, especially those which are concerned with humanitarian projects, and, as a permanent member of the Security Council, Britain could use its veto to support positive action and maybe even hold the United States in check when it attempted to railroad its own policies through. All this would save enormous sums of money that would be available for increased international aid and still leave more for our hard-pressed public services and pensioners.

It would be absurd to suggest that such a radical departure from post-war dependence on and subservience to American policy diktats could be achieved easily, not least because it would also undermine the claim by a succession of prime ministers to be world leaders, which would weaken their authority at home. However, none of these reasons should discourage us from arguing, publicly, the case for these policies. Such a campaign might well win a lot of public support, both here and in the United States itself, where many Americans share our anxieties and hopes.

21 December 2001

Nuclear power and the bomb

The future of nuclear power is back on the agenda as the government reconsiders its future in the energy review. The outcome is of great importance for all of us since it is so closely linked to nuclear weapons.

During the war, Harold Nicolson wrote a novel called *Public Faces*, in which he described the invention of an atom bomb by Britain. Thus the news of the atomic attack on Hiroshima seemed rather like a fantasy that had come true. Group Captain Leonard Cheshire, who was sent as the Cabinet representative in one of the planes which were involved in that raid, told a student meeting I later attended that if we did not get our policy on nuclear weapons right, everything else we were doing was a complete waste of time.

In 1955 President Eisenhower launched the 'Atoms for Peace' programme. Many people, including me, saw this as a classic example of 'beating swords into ploughshares' and strongly supported civil nuclear power in Britain – a view I still held when in 1966 I was appointed Minister of Technology, with responsibility for the development of that programme.

I was told, believed and argued publicly that civil nuclear power was cheap, safe and peaceful. It was only later that I learned that this was all untrue since if the full cost of development and the cost of storing long-term nuclear waste is included in the calculations nuclear power is three times more expensive than coal. (I learned this when the pits were being closed on economic grounds.)

Nuclear power is certainly not safe, as we know from accidents at Windscale (now renamed Sellafield), Three-Mile Island in America and Chernobyl in the Ukraine. Nevertheless, the authorities have always been determined to downplay the dangers. Nor are Britain's civil nuclear power stations entirely peaceful in their purpose, as for many years – and still possibly today – the plutonium they produced was sent to fuel the American nuclear weapons programme, making them, in effect, bomb factories.

As Minister of Technology, at no stage could I rely on being told the truth, either by the industry itself or by my own civil servants (who may or may not have known it themselves). Some dramatic examples of misinformation that made a deep impression on me converted me from being a supporter to a very strong opponent of the whole nuclear power programme.

Once, in Japan, a Japanese minister asked me how we were getting on with the task of clearing after up the fire at Windscale years before, of which I was wholly unaware. When I raised this with my officials they replied that as it had occurred before I took office they had not wanted to 'bother me' with it. All this was at a time when I was arguing that nuclear power was safe. The same excuse, that it was 'before my time', was offered when I discovered that stolen plutonium had gone to Israel to form the basis of that country's atomic weapons programme.

Most serious of all, I heard from the chairman of the Atomic Energy Authority (AEA) that when in 1957 the Soviet reprocessing plant at Kyshtym had a major accident, the CIA, which had picked this up on their own monitoring system, notified the AEA, but told them not to tell British ministers in case it shook public confidence in nuclear power. This was offered as the reason why I had not been informed.

It was only after the 1979 election that I heard from a senior scientist in the generating board, that while I was actually a minister – and unknown to me – plutonium from our civil nuclear power stations was being sent to America for the US military programme.

Nuclear power is in fact expensive, dangerous and all about the bomb. The generation of electricity is used as a cover to mislead the public so that the arms programme can be munitioned.

The decision to proceed with the MOX fuel plant at Sellafield against the strong opposition of the Irish and Norwegian governments, which fear radioactive discharges, suggests that the Prime Minister is determined to go ahead with nuclear power, although the German government has decided to decommission nineteen of its nuclear reactors.

Interestingly, the original plan in the United States, to build 2000 reactors by the year 2000 was dropped years ago because of public opposition to their construction. This may well be the reason why Britain supplied America with the plutonium which it needed.

Another problem with nuclear power was the secret and unhealthy link between senior British officials and Westinghouse, who were busy trying to persuade us to start a massive new power station programme using their own pressure water reactor, which I had been advised had potential safety problems.

Throughout this long saga I came to know, trust and work with Friends of the Earth, Greenpeace and other committed environmentalists whose expert advice was generously made available and led me to change my mind on the issue.

So when we learn the outcome of the review, these are factors we must keep in mind, because you can be sure that if the decision to go ahead is made we will not be told the whole truth, and military links with the United States may well be the real reason behind it.

11 January 2002

Money for votes

The attempt by the European Central Bank to censure Chancellor Gordon Brown for his plans to invest public money in the public services, together with the threat, now withdrawn, to impose a fine on Chancellor Schröder for exceeding the approved limit for public expenditure (in part forced by the high level of unemployment in Germany), is a stark reminder of what joining the euro means for Europe, and what it would really mean for us.

After all the hype about the new euro currency, and how exciting it is and how convenient it would be for British holidaymakers on the Continent if Britain joins, the real issue has at last surfaced. It is about the total loss of democratic control of our economy which we would experience if we did opt for the new currency.

The Maastricht Treaty, which we have already signed, lays down, under the so-called 'stability pact', the limits of borrowing and spending that are permitted in every country which ratified the treaty. Although we have not signed up to the euro itself we are still subject to the same rules, which is why we are being forced to undergo an extensive programme of privatization.

The second problem that will soon have to be confronted by countries in the eurozone is that they will all be subject to the same interest rates also set by the Central Bank. It should be obvious that conditions vary from country to country, and that a set rate may be too high in one country and too low in another, which might have disastrous results that could not be corrected.

The Maastricht Treaty also makes it an offence for any government even to try to influence the decisions of the Central Bank. Thus if German, French, Italian, Spanish or British trade unionists, or even industrialists, were to appeal to their own elected governments to reduce interest rates in order to save jobs, the finance ministers of the governments they have elected would be unable to do so.

This in turn would undermine all public confidence in the democratic process because if the parliaments we elect are powerless, then why should anyone bother to vote? If they don't vote, that is the end of democracy itself, and the way is open for some demagogue to take over.

Inevitably people here who were suffering would look for a scapegoat. It would be much easier to whip up hostility to the Germans or the French than to understand the real nature of the problem, which would be that the system itself was at fault.

And the dangers would not step there. The discovery that we were governed by bankers we did not elect and could not remove would inevitably lead to the crudest form of nationalism. I can even visualize a breakdown in Europe along the lines of that in former Yugoslavia, with all the subsequent consequences.

Of course Europe must cooperate for the benefit of all its peoples, and the wider world, but that cooperation must be based on a democratic process that underpins and entrenches the rights of all its citizens to govern themselves through their own elected parliaments, harmonizing their policies slowly and by consent in line with the wide variations in the conditions that each face.

It is not clear when, or even if, a referendum will be called to determine whether Britain should join the euro. If the Prime Minister called a referendum and lost it – as well he might – this could spell the end of his government and a very uncertain future, but we must be ready for that debate.

I suspect, without any inside knowledge of any kind, that no Chancellor of the Exchequer could possibly want to give up the power he has to control our own economy. Likewise, no Governor of the Bank of England would want to see his own role downgraded to that of a mere branch manager, taking all his orders from head office in Frankfurt.

What is of the most immediate importance to those of

us in the Labour movement is how we can persuade some influential trade union leaders who now support the euro to realize that they are cutting their own throats by doing so, in that they could not influence the government they support because that government would be utterly powerless too.

Put very crudely, the euro question is fundamental to whether we still believe in democracy itself, or whether we have abandoned it, entrusting our future to bankers who do not share our objectives and are determined to control us in the interest of capital. For they will use deflation as the simplest way of weakening Labour to boost profits for their real constituents – the shareholders of Europe and the world.

If ever there were a case for studying history as a guide to the future then this is it, and the neglect of our own history in the Labour movement is a major tragedy that we have it in our power to correct. Anyone who looks back on how the trade unions came into being, fought for and won the vote and then developed a political wing to improve the conditions of their own members through parliament must see that we have to do it all over again. And those who remember, or bother to read about, the history of the 1930s will realize that it was the despair caused by the policy of the bankers which paved the way for Hitler and Mussolini and then took us into war.

Meanwhile, a simple tip for holidaymakers to the Continent: any British banker's card will today dish out euros in any bank in Europe, without us having to give up our democracy here at home.

15 February 2002

Time for a change?

This is a time when we should be thinking very hard about what is going on, before we are swept forward into another war and the acceptance of policies that could damage the whole fabric of our society and destroy what it has taken many years to build up.

This week Vice-President Cheney has been in London explaining to the Prime Minister why, when and how President Bush is planning to attack Iraq, and instructing him as to the role that Britain must play in support (including the provision of up to 25,000 troops for that operation).

We now know that in addition to the so-called 'Axis of Evil' – Iraq, Iran and North Korea – listed by Bush a few weeks ago, the White House has actually decided that China and Russia should now be identified as suitable targets for nuclear attacks.

Indeed, it is beginning to become apparent that the greatest threat to world peace may not really be individual terrorists but the US administration itself, yet, judging by the statements issued by Downing Street, the Prime Minister is offering his full support once he can persuade the public to back this war, which is why the media is now busy brainwashing us into the acceptance of the bloodshed still to come by publishing and broadcasting all the propaganda supplied by the Pentagon.

Indeed, despite our own relatively minor military strength the Prime Minister appears to have persuaded himself that if he does everything he is told to do by Bush he can behave as if he was in charge of a revived British Empire. (He must have influenced the Prince of Wales to criticize President Mugabe for the way he has conducted the elections in Zimbabwe, without mentioning the fact that he himself will become king by inheritance.) Perhaps the most serious piece of self-deception is the Prime Minister's belief that he exercises a restraining influence on the President. This is a complete illusion, since Bush has no intention of allowing anyone – neither the UN, NATO nor the EU to tell him what to do.

All this goes on despite Britain's treaty obligations to the UN Charter, the opposition of Kofi Annan, the UN Secretary-General, and Mr Blair's own commitment to the organization in the revised Clause 4 of Labour's constitution, forced through in 1995.

Before we believe what we are told we should note the recent report from Washington that the Pentagon has set up a covert unit to wage an information war that could include feeding false stories to foreign media. One senior official is quoted as saying that the propaganda battle 'goes from the blackest of black propaganda to the whitest of white', which should alert us to the likelihood that what we read and see may just be a deliberate lie invented and intended to deceive us.

Labour opposition to this war is strong and growing, and those MPs who have signed a motion against it almost certainly represent a clear majority, both in the party and the country. When the killing starts, the peace movement has a crucial role in building up a really strong campaign, just as is happening in America where a peace march on Washington is planned for 20 April.

But it is not only against the war that Labour is stirring, as we know from John Monks who, in a major speech last week, warned the government that unless it took trade union concerns about manufacturing industy, privatization and pensions seriously, its support could haemorrhage, with fatal damage to its prospects of re-election. For steel jobs in Wales are already threatened by the new US tariffs on imports from Britain. The privatization of our public services is proceeding fast. Moreover, many pensioners now face poverty in old age after a lifetime of work that gave us the security we now enjoy.

In Germany, almost half the local authorities are being forced to sell off hospital clinics, libraries and swimming pools to pay their bills, driven by budget deficits running into billions of pounds. This is what Mr Blair wants here too.

So great is the gap that has opened up between New Labour and Labour voters that the Liberal leader Charles Kennedy and even John Bercow, the Conservative front-bencher, have spoken of ways in which they could fill the role of being friendly to the unions.

It is true that the radical Liberals or old one-nation Tories were, in some respects, far more progressive than New Labour is, and the present opposition leaders might decide to move to the Left for tactical reasons, just as the Prime Minister moved to the Right as soon as he became party leader in 1994.

This possibility needs to be kept in mind when we are threatened with letting the Tories in if we do not accept everything the Prime Minister wants us to do. That is not the real alternative, which would be a Labour Government.

Over the last few days, a handful of Labour MPs have been quietly talking about what that would mean and how it could be achieved. It is worth remembering that at the time of the Suez war in 1956, when Nasser was being compared to Hitler, Hugh Gaitskell, then the Labour leader, denounced Sir Anthony Eden for his aggression against Egypt and, when it failed, Prime Minister Eden was driven out of office and replaced by another Tory.

Could it happen to a Labour leader?

15 March 2002

A state of Palestine now

The main responsibility for the appalling crimes being perpetrated against the Palestinians must be equally shared between Jerusalem and Washington, for successive American governments have funded Israel, armed Israel and used their veto at the Security Council to protect Israel from being forced to comply with what world opinion wanted it to do.

In defence of his brutal and cruel policy of occupation and persecution Sharon has turned on his critics and accused them of anti-semitism, almost as if Arafat was some modern-day Hitler preparing a new Holocaust against a weak and terrified people, deserted by the world.

Such a charge is itself gross and obscene and flies in the face of all the facts, some of which need to be recalled. Not least among these is the fact that America did not enter the war until the attack on Pearl Harbor, and without that precipitating factor might never have done so, although by that time the Nazi persecution of the Jews was well known.

Many of today's sternest critics of Israel's present

aggression welcomed the foundation of the state, looking to the prospect of peace between the Jews and Palestinians when that was achieved. I was one of them, having been staying on leave, as a serviceman, on a kibbutz by the Sea of Galilee in 1945 when the Germans surrendered. We danced all night with Jews from all over Europe who had found their way to Palestine as refugees.

Later, at a conference in Tel Aviv organized by MAPAM, a Jewish socialist party, on the prospects of peace, I joined with others as we discussed how such cooperation could be built and how the Palestinians might be able to return to their homes from which they had been driven.

But of course the Suez conspiracy with Britain and France gave Israel a chance to extend her boundaries, as did the Six-Day War. It was then that the UN called for a return to the original frontiers, leaving the Palestinians room to set up their own state in what in law was land still belonging to the Jordanians. However, this never happened because America would not permit it.

Seeing Israel as a valuable base for the extension of US power in the Middle East, Washington put such pressure on their client states in Saudi Arabia and Egypt that none of them was prepared to recognize a new Palestine. Israel took advantage of that to build huge towns for Israelis – known as settlements – deep inside the Palestinian areas, while still denying exiled Palestinians the right to return to their own homes in Israel.

So hostile was Washington to Arafat himself that when the UN called him to give evidence he was denied a visa to enter the United States, and the UN session had to be moved to Geneva. The so-called peace process, which

Bush now pretends to be encouraging, is a complete fraud, designed only to keep the Arab states quiet in preparation for his real war against Iraq.

The British role in all this over the years has been less than honest, in that we have supplied arms to Israel and all too often joined the United States in giving the Israelis the support they demanded. However, now the crisis has reached such gravity, we should insist that our government act firmly and independently.

Obviously it must be for Arafat to decide how to move, but if, even from his besieged bunker, he were to declare to the world that a state of Palestine has been set up in the territory laid down by the UN, and appeal for recognition by the Security Council and all friendly nations, the situation could be transformed. Israeli troops would by that very fact alone be transformed from being the 'forces of law and order', which is how Sharon likes to present them, into what they really are – an army of occupation in a neighbouring state which they have attacked in an act of aggression against international law.

Britain should offer its support for this strategy by stopping all arms sales to Israel, introducing trade sanctions and a ban on all investment there, together with a boycott of Israeli goods here, and make it a condition for the lifting of these measures that Israel complies with these demands at once.

The massive demonstration in support of Palestine that took place in Trafalgar Square last Saturday was one of the largest that I have seen. It must have been encouraging for the Muslims who organized it that so many people from the British Labour and peace movements came to express their solidarity.

Predictably, the mass media either ignored or gave only the briefest of coverage to that demonstration. They focused their cameras on the burning of one American flag without reporting a word of what was said from the platform, when we all know that the views expressed there command the backing of the overwhelming majority of the population of the world.

American hostility to Arafat and support for Sharon is what is prolonging the tragedy, as thousands of Palestinians are suffering death and injury from military action which they cannot resist in kind but can defeat by their determination and courage if we can help from outside.

Every sort of pressure must now be brought to bear on the Prime Minister so that he is left in no doubt of the anger that he has stirred here at his continuing subservience to Bush in this and every other policy that the President lays down. If we are to avoid a world war the government had better rethink its own position, and do so very quickly.

19 April 2002

Isolating the isolationists

After George Washington, a highly successful terrorist leader, led the American colonies to independence in a long and bitter war against George III, he announced that as president he did not want his country to get involved in any 'entangling alliances', and that phrase marked the birth of American isolationism.

That position was reasserted after the First World War, when the Senate overwhelmingly refused to ratify the charter of the League of Nations. It thus exempted itself from playing any role in the attempt – which ultimately failed – to build some sort of an international order to replace the balance of power which had marked earlier efforts to regulate international conduct by the European powers.

Isolationism was the policy of the United States throughout the 1920s and 1930s, when fascism and Nazism came to dominate Europe. When the Second World War began, in 1939, the United States stayed out of the conflict, taking the position of a neutral.

As late as May 1941, just before Hitler launched his attack on the Soviet Union, Senator Truman, later president himself and the founder of NATO, said that if the Germans seemed to be winning the United States should support the Russians, and if the Russians seemed to be winning it should support the Germans, in the hope that as many as possible on both sides would be killed.

Roosevelt, who was very sympathetic to Churchill, was unable to take America into the war because of the isolationist majority, and indeed after the Japanese attacked Pearl Harbor in 1941 Germany and Italy declared war on America before Congress itself had been able to declare war.

But when the war ended, the Senate ratified the UN Charter with no serious opposition, and the UN was established in New York to underline the commitment of America to its work.

American forces remained in Europe after the end of the war. They were accepted by Britain, France and West Germany, partly for fear of a Soviet invasion and partly to commit the United States to Europe for the foreseeable future. When NATO was established the first article in its own charter pledged loyalty to that of the UN. Even when the American forces were sent into Korea, Washington did this under the flag of the UN by getting the General Assembly to pass a resolution called 'United for Peace'.

In recent years, however, this commitment to the UN has completely disappeared, since the wars against Yugoslavia and Afghanistan had no UN mandate. Neither do the no-fly zones in Iraq, breaches of which are used to justify regular bombing of that country by the United States.

With the adoption of 'Full Spectrum Dominance' and the Star Wars project, which would allow the United States to destroy any land installation in the world by laser-beams from space, America has began to withdraw from its international obligations, including the UN and the anti-ballistic missile treaty. NATO itself has been sidelined because Europe is not regarded as reliable.

America is so powerful that it believes it can act on its own, wherever and whenever it wishes, to protect its interests without regard to international law. It has listed 60 nations where intervention would (in its view) be justified and identified others that are 'evil'. The rest of the world is expected to accept all this as the beginning of a new Pax Americana.

Given the overwhelming military power that Bush wields with weapons of mass destruction of all kinds, including biological and chemical weapons, and the industrial and economic power that underpins it all, there is nothing – at the moment – that anyone can do to prevent US acts of aggression from taking place.

But we do not have to accept this situation. America

must expect a response from across the world that takes that into account, as more countries realize that their alliance with the United States is both unnecessary and undesirable and should be terminated.

Why, we might ask, now the Cold War is over, do we need American bases in Britain? Who is the enemy from whom we are being protected? Last but not least, are we ready to see airfields and intelligence bases here used by the White House for wars with which we disagree?

In short, the time has come to reopen the whole question of all US bases, including Fylingdales and Menwith Hill, and begin once again the campaign to have them closed, especially as we know that the President regards Britain as an unsinkable aircraft carrier from which he can launch his deadly attacks on any enemy he chooses (as happened in the Gulf War and in the bombing of Libya).

No system purporting to defend law and order can win without the consent of those who are supposed to benefit. A new world order that is likely to be durable must be based upon consent and not coercion. The fact is that American coercion of any nation will inevitably fail, as all coercive strategies have done in the past, but we can best bring that home to Washington by withdrawing our consent to their use of our land for their wars.

Even if Britain demanded the withdrawal of all US bases here I do not believe for a moment that the United States would go along with this. However, from that moment, Britain would be seen as an occupied country, and there are many Americans who would not like to be seen as citizens of an occupying power. Nevertheless, until the Americans manage to bring about a regime change in Washington we are all in deep trouble, and we must work closely with all those progressive people in the United States who share that objective.

9 August 2002

Johannesburg and Washington

The choice facing the human race, upon which its very survival may depend, has been brought into clear focus this week by events taking place in Washington, the capital of the richest and most powerful empire the world has ever seen, and Johannesburg, where some of the poorest people in the world live. Washington is openly preparing for war and Johannesburg is trying, hesitantly, to chart a route leading to the establishment of universal justice, without which peace is not possible.

In America the decision to go to war will be made by one man, funded by, and representing, the financial interests of the richest corporations that now exploit the planet for profit. He will be acting without even the authority of the elected Congress and in defiance of the Charter of the UN. In Africa the Secretary-General of the UN, in the spirit of its Charter, is seeking consensus among all the nations there represented to agree upon policies that inevitably would, and certainly should, shift the balance of world power in favour of the poor at the expense of the rich. If Bush goes to war tens of thousands of innocent people will die, and if Kofi Annan succeeds tens of millions of people, now facing sickness and an early death, will survive.

If the population of the world were able to vote between a war against Iraq and the prospect of sustainable development, the result would be more than 99.9 per cent for peace and a mere handful hoping to make a quick buck out of war.

If these were not sufficient arguments to persuade the Prime Minister to distance himself from the President, important practical arguments against this war of aggression can also be deployed, and these relate to the consequences that would follow in the Middle East. For though the White House claims that Iraq poses a threat to the region, not a single nation that borders on it will back the war because they know what would happen if they did. No one doubts that with its overwhelming military strength America could destroy Iraq by using the methods of mass destruction which it possesses, but that hardware will be no good if the conflict spreads, as it might, to Egypt or Saudi Arabia, or brings in Israel, with its own nuclear weapons.

Bush hopes that we will forget the massive military backing given by earlier US presidents to Saddam Hussein when he fought the long and bloody war against Iran, including visits to Baghdad by Donald Rumsfeld to negotiate US support and even supply chemical weapons that were used on Kurds.

In that Iran–Iraq war one of the issues was the extent to which militant Muslims should be allowed to determine the policy of a nation, as happened in Tehran after the Iranian revolution which overthrew the Shah – an American puppet – and brought Ayatollah Khomeini to power committed to the strict application of Muslim law.

Saddam Hussein and his Ba'athist party were totally opposed to the Iranian revolution. It was his opposition that earned him the backing of the Americans, which makes it even more absurd to suggest that Saddam has any sympathy with the al-Qa'eda network or was responsible for what happened on September 11.

Indeed, it was the Americans who tried to use extreme Muslim groups to undermine communism during the Cold War, as in Afghanistan. Even two years ago the CIA knew quite well that Osama bin Laden's group was secretly backing the Kosovo Liberation Army in its war against former Yugoslavia.

Blair has made his decision to stand shoulder to shoulder with Bush, and Bush has said that 'anyone who is not with us is against us' – a sinister warning that even close friends who query any aspect of the White House policy are 'soft on terrorism' and would pay a price for that.

Yet now a whole host of very distinguished Americans have been urging caution. It was for fear that this might be mobilizing opinion in the United States for peace that the Vice-president was wheeled out, a day or two ago, to make it clear that war was already decided and in active preparation. The return of the arms inspectors had nothing to do with it and, with inside knowledge, he added that he was sure Britain would back the war.

The choice Britain has to make at this moment is therefore of absolutely critical significance, not only for all the reasons given above, but because of the impact it could well have on the future of the Labour Party and the Labour movement. If resolutions condemning this war can be tabled and carried at the TUC and Labour conferences, the Prime Minister would be passing a death-sentence on many innocent people now living in Iraq and defying the party he leads on a fundamental issue. For the prosecution of this war would amount to a deliberate act of destruction, with consequences that could only harm the interests of all those the Labour movement was set up to protect.

That is why we need an enormous campaign aimed at persuading delegates to vote against war, despite all the threats to which they will be subjected and the false suggestion that no decision has been made – when we all know that it has, although the exact date when the attack is to be launched has yet to be decided.

We must demand that the UN Security Council and the House of Commons should both be recalled to debate the situation and that no decision be taken without the wholehearted consent of both, in line with our obligations under the UN Charter.

30 August 2002

6

Trade Unions and Privatization

Selling our future

Public opinion is now building up very strongly against the policy of privatization which the government is determined to push through. Whether it is dressed up as a public–private partnership for the London Underground or as the private finance initiative for hospitals and schools, most people can see exactly what it really is – the selling-off of our public services and the transfer of many of those who work in them to a market-based system.

When in opposition Labour attacked the Tories most vigorously for their privatization measures, voting against all of them, yet now it is in government it is carrying the process far further.

The Treasury commitment to privatization is based on the provisions of the Maastricht Treaty, which binds all signatory countries to restrict their public expenditure. If Britain were to join the euro the total control of our economic policy would pass from parliament to the Central Bank in Frankfurt.

Given these restrictions, the Chancellor argues that the only way of paying for the improvements we need without increasing public expenditure is to harness private capital. However, the real reason is that if this was done by public investment Britain could never join the euro.

In the past, publicly owned enterprises such as British Nuclear Fuel and the British National Oil Corporation were free to borrow on the market to finance their expansion without losing 100 per cent public control or including these loans in public expenditure – and at a far lower cost. That is the case for a bond issue for the London Underground, for which Ken Livingstone has been campaigning. Treasury opposition to this is complete nonsense.

Underlying all this is the determination of the WTO to press ahead with its plan to open up all the world's services to private capital under a new general agreement on trade in services, which would permit multinational corporations to take over hospitals and schools everywhere and make enormous profits at our expense.

Far from representing a policy of modernization this would be a throwback to the early nineteenth century before the welfare services began under the new elected local authorities brought into being by the Municipal Corporations Act of 1837. Using the powers given them under that Act, Birmingham, for example, established a huge range of services including municipal schools, hospitals, fire and police, housing, gas, electricity, transport, libraries and museums. In this way people who could not afford to buy their house, educate their children or get private medical care were able to have access to these services by voting for councillors who would provide them. This marked the birth of the Welfare State – long before the Labour Party itself was born. The policy also guaranteed that those who ran these services would be accountable for what they did – which is quite impossible under privatization.

Those who are now affected by the privatization we already have are well aware that their own wages and working conditions have worsened and that trade unions have been put under pressure to go along with whatever their new bosses want to do. Ask the Dudley Hospital workers who are on strike, or the rail workers in London about safety under private ownership, and it is clear how strong the feeling is.

Everyone in the Labour movement should be giving their full support to the campaigns to stop privatization. At a very well-attended conference held in London last Saturday, speakers from RMT, ASLEF, PCS, Unison and the FBU all argued the need for solidarity.

At this very moment the trade unions have a key role to play, because if they were to insist that Labour's election manifesto, to be published next month, must contain a pledge to halt all privatization, then the government could not go ahead with this policy. If, on the other hand, out of a misplaced sense of loyalty the union representatives on the manifesto committee do not take a stand, then the campaign will have to be taken up after the election and fought very hard.

For what is at stake here is nothing less than the survival of the public services, publicly funded and publicly accountable, and the democratic process itself. For if the WTO and the European Central Bank can take over our lives in a pincer operation then we could lose everything.

Having said all that, I am certain that the private finance initiative and the policy of privatization can be stopped. Our role must be to support those who are now taking action and win the argument with the wider public, who may not yet realize exactly what is at stake.

6 April 2001

Selling off the Post Office

Tom Sawyer's report on the state of industrial relations in the Post Office, as reported in the *Morning Star*, identified the 'high-handed, insensitive' management which had caused many industrial disputes, while *The Times*, under a headline 'Royal Mail on brink of collapse', implied that customers 'are likely to turn to private-sector competitors when they become available'.

Given the government's deep commitment to privatization it is easy to see how the Prime Minister might want to use this report to justify a decision to sell off the Post Office, and the process of dismantling Britain's oldest public service has already begun.

Mrs Thatcher privatized the telephone service and sold off the Giro, and now we have to face the demands from the EU that the monopoly powers of the Post Office should be weakened in order to open up the service to competition from private carriers.

The Royal Mail is now owned by a holding company renamed Consignia, which was justified on the grounds that it sounded more trendy in the age of the logo. In fact, the renaming was done to make it harder for people to see what was really happening and to arrange a sale without anyone noticing. (This also occurred when British Steel was renamed Corus and sacked thousands of its workers with impunity.)

Despite all the denials that have come from ministers, I suspect that the Royal Mail will be quietly disposed of. This will probably be justified on the grounds that in the age of global business the idea of a national service is out of date, and that the EU should have its own postal system, preferably run by a private corporation.

The Royal Mail was originally set up in 1660 by King Charles II. His motive was crude in the extreme: it was to allow him to open everyone's letters and keep an eye on possible trouble. It was, to all intents and purposes, the birth of MI5, and something of that element is still persists today.

Up until the 1840s letters were charged according to the distance they had to travel, but when Rowland Hill – a genuine and committed public servant – took over the postal system, he realized that the cost lay not in distance but in handling, and he introduced the standard penny post which applied across the whole country.

This was a revolution indeed, copied all over the world – as was the British postage stamp. It made possible a massive growth of popular communication, in its time comparable to what the Internet is doing today, carrying letters, postcards and parcels providing for printed material to go all over the country.

It was, and still is, a genuine public service which allows those who lived in remote areas to get their letters at the same rate as city-dwellers, even though the cost of rural deliveries is far, far higher. This is made possible by a system of internal subsidy which benefits us all. Later, in the same spirit of public service, the GPO decided to handle material for the blind (much heavier in weight because of bulky Braille) absolutely free, which is the best example you could imagine of what only a public service can do.

And at the beginning of the last century it was a Liberal government which nationalized the National Telephone Company and brought that service under the wing of the GPO, where it grew at a great rate, and provided call-boxes in remote areas where no private company would have regarded them as economic.

In Harold Wilson's first Labour government, the Giro Bank was launched, along with the National Data Processing Service. Some postal buses were also launched to allow people in remote rural areas to have access to transport on GPO vehicles. It was decided to free the Post Office from Treasury control, which had tended to stifle innovation, and the telephone service was converted into a public corporation, 100 per cent publicly owned, and able to expand much more rapidly.

Admittedly the GPO was once run in a rather autocratic way, with almost military discipline, but the Union of Post Office Workers (UPW) was committed to the idea of guild socialism, which is really a form of industrial democracy.

All these achievements are now at risk because of the Prime Minister's obvious hostility to all forms of public enterprise and trade unionism and his passion for deregulation, free trade, globalization and market forces at whatever cost to those who work in the service or depend upon it.

At the TUC and Labour Party conferences, which take place next month, it is open to trade union and constituency delegates to make clear our belief in public service provision and reject the policy of privatization which the government seeks to impose.

Charles Clarke, who has been appointed to the non-existent and non-elected post of Chairman of the Labour Party, has told us that the government intends to get its way whatever the party conference decides. However, if that threat is to be taken seriously it suggests that New Labour wants to be rid of the Labour Party itself – and that we cannot accept.

Because of the failure of unregulated market forces, a world recession is slowly creeping up on us which could cause great hardship and suffering for those we represent. This is a time when the Labour movement must stand firm and not abandon its historic mission to safeguard the interests of working people.

3 August 2001

The legacy of Jimmy Knapp

Last Monday the Labour movement turned out in force for the requiem mass in Chiswick to celebrate the life of railway leader Jimmy Knapp. It was a very moving occasion.

Almost every seat was taken half an hour before the service began. By the time the coffin entered, the church was packed to the doors with people who knew and loved Jimmy standing all around, determined to be there to pay their own tribute.

There were readings by Vernon Hince and Tony Dubbins, and prayers read by Rodney Bickerstaffe. The service ended with a brilliant, perceptive and amusing eulogy from John Monks, who captured the feelings of all those who were there. Everyone clapped, almost as if we had all been at a political rally.

The congregation was made up of those who knew him and worked with him. There were many veterans of the trade union movement, including Jack Jones, Ron Todd, Norman Willis, Ken Cameron, Tony Clarke, Ken Gill, Frank Cave and Sid Greene. The present generation was represented by Bill Morris, John Edmonds and Mick Rix.

In short, it was the Labour movement itself, gathered to remember an old comrade on the eve of the most important TUC for years, which meets next month to chart out its programme for the future and restate its own commitment to the causes which brought it into existence.

Funerals have an important role in the life of our movement because, apart from the grief we want to express, they offer us an opportunity to recall the life's work of those who have died and learn the lessons for our own work in the future, and that is exactly what happened on Monday.

The media often describe our political debates in terms of a conflict by setting those who are loyal to our leaders against trouble-makers, moderates against extremists, pragmatists against ideologues, or realists against idealists. So it is necessary to recall the solid achievement of those who devote their lives to the service of their members, guided by their own experience and beliefs, and who make big progress in little incremental steps.

Jimmy, now widely recognized as a great and wise leader, was regularly denounced by right-wing politicians and leader-writers in a press for which trade unionism itself is inherently subversive and hostile to the public interest.

Now, with the benefit of hindsight, the overwhelming majority of the public have learned by experience why we need a publicly owned, publicly financed and publicly accountable railway system, committed to the interests both of its own staff and passengers who want to know that safety comes first.

One reason why the trade unions are now beginning to feel more confident is that they sense, as we all do, that the things for which trade unionism stands are what the nation feels it needs.

Trade unions want to represent people, while governments want to manage them. There is all the difference in the world between those two interpretations of leadership, which may explain why trade union membership is rising and votes for New Labour have been falling.

Standing around talking to all my old mates after the service it was obvious that they recognize the responsibility that now rests upon their shoulders: not just to be effective union members but also to be more active in the political work of the party. A few to whom I spoke expressed their concern at the direction New Labour has taken and sounded a bit gloomy, but others had picked up the new and more determined mood that is discernible at the grassroots, feeling as excited as I do at the new possibilities for advance that are now opening up.

John Monks reminded us that an older generation tackled problems far more difficult than the ones we have to face, as when he compared Jimmy to the pioneers going back to the Tolpuddle Martyrs. All in all, I got the feeling that everyone who was there knew what had to be done at Brighton next month, when key issues of policy come up for decision at the TUC and Labour conferences.

History is beginning to turn full circle. What we stand for, which is representation, a vision of a better future and a strong united organization to make it possible, is the only way to restore public confidence in the democratic process and make it work for this generation, as it has done for those who have gone before us.

What Britain needs is so simple: secure and worthwhile jobs at decent wages with good conditions; public services for all, including housing and education; health-care for all and dignity in retirement; and we know that globalization and market forces cannot deliver these for us.

Those of us in the Labour movement are also internationalists; we want an end to discrimination, to racism and the arms race, which could destroy life on earth. Jimmy believed passionately in all these things, and that is why he inspired us all throughout his life.

24 August 2001

Pride in the public services

The warning by OFSTED's Chief Inspector of Schools that the teacher shortage is now more serious than it has been at any time since 1960 could well undermine the government's much-vaunted emphasis on the importance of education. There are important lessons to be learned here if our public services are to meet the growing needs of our society.

Public services must be properly funded, past neglect having left us with huge problems. The housing crisis for teachers and nurses in many urban areas has highlighted the need for good low-cost accommodation, which is fast becoming hard to find. Pay is another factor. It tends to be higher in the private sector, and this may explain why some people move when a better-paid job appears.

But there is another factor that cannot be disregarded and that is morale in the public services. This has been seriously damaged by the practice of 'naming and shaming' schools and hospitals which have experienced difficulties that may have had nothing whatever to do with the quality of those who work in them. Thus people who are struggling to do well, and who are well aware of the problems they face, are subjected to unnecessary stress and anxiety. Giving encouragement and support is the surest way to get the best out of people. If they feel that their work is appreciated it creates pride and self-confidence without which no one can be expected to perform well.

It is also strange that this process of naming and shaming has not been followed in ministerial comments on the activities of the private sector, despite the disgraceful way in which workers have been treated when redundancies have been announced or when environmental issues have been ignored in business decisions or when consumers get a raw deal.

We are told that this is a business-friendly government, and that those who criticize private companies may damage investment. Why, we may ask, can we not have a government that boasts that it is equally friendly to the public sector? I am afraid that this double standard conceals a different agenda at the top, and that the attacks on the public services are really motivated by a desire to accommodate us to the necessity of privatization and to give that policy a fig-leaf of respectability.

Certainly, the contemptuous reference to 'bog-standard comprehensives' was intended to justify the return of selection. This may explain why some schools are being handed over to private companies to run – a development that could be extended to privatize elected LEAs.

Council housing stock is also being sold off, which could well make the provision of low-cost houses even more difficult. The fiasco of the London Underground privatization is being put forward as the government's answer to the virtual collapse of public transport – caused by years of underinvestment – in that city.

Obviously the public services need much more money, but there is absolutely no reason why this cannot be raised by the Treasury issuing bonds or inviting private investment in wholly owned public corporations, as in the case of the British National Oil Company, which attracted funds from all over the world.

Difficulties in the public services can best be overcome by asking those who actually work in them (and therefore know them well), to suggest necessary improvements, rather than hiring new layers of management and deliberately trying to damage the morale of those whose efforts will be needed to make things work.

Years ago, when I was in Cuba, I visited the hospital in Havana and, at my request, they explained how it was run. There were three meetings every month. The first of these, which was chaired by the management and attended by the unions and the government, discussed practical organizational issues. The second meeting, chaired by the unions and attended by the management and the government, allowed the problems facing the staff to be raised. The third meeting, chaired by the government, with management and unions present, addressed the role of the hospital within the national health-care strategy. It was by far the most democratic system I have ever come across, and the effect on morale was obvious and must partially explain why Cuba has a far higher standard of health-care than is available in the immensely rich United States, where it is all in private hands.

Cuban education also gives that small country higher standards than in America. It provides a hugely successful service, including the training of doctors for the developing world.

We believe in the public services because we recognize the skill and commitment of those who work in them as their greatest asset which we must cherish, encourage and develop to the full.

Ministers would do well to stop sniping at the public services and ask a few more questions about big business and how it treats its employees here and world-wide.

31 August 2001

Key role for the unions

All the obituaries to Moss Evans have referred to the so-called 'Winter of Discontent' and the role he and the TGWU played at that time, attributing the defeat of the Labour government to what he and the other unions did then. This is so central a part of the political mythology of the period that very few people can now remember that two years earlier, in 1976, the IMF put tremendous pressure on the Cabinet to make major cuts in public expenditure, threatening to undermine the value of the pound sterling if it refused to do so. The Cabinet gave way, but in fact, the figures given to it were wrong, as Denis Healey, then Chancellor, has with characteristic honesty since admitted. If the oil reserves had been added to the gold and dollar reserves – as I requested – it would have revealed the immense strength of our underlying economy, and the cuts would not have been needed.

In point of fact, cuts were not needed anyway. The IMF's real purpose in all this was to undermine the Labour government, in the hope that the Tories could return to power – which they did.

Given the cuts, it was both inevitable – and right – for the unions to take action to protect their members' interests. I recall Moss Evans explaining why the TGWU broke the 5 per cent pay limit in his negotiations with Ford. Ford, he told us, could well afford a higher settlement than had been laid down by the government, because the company had made a big profit out of the higher productivity of his members. Had he accepted the 5 per cent on offer, the extra money would not have gone to help the teachers, the nurses or the low-paid; rather, it would have gone straight into the pockets of the Ford shareholders. Moreover, he added, we were only allowed to bargain on pay, whereas if we had been able to say to Ford 'we will accept a lower wage increase if you will use the money to cut the price of Ford cars or invest in a new engine plant in Britain', the TGWU might well have settled.

It was the IMF – not the unions – which gave a victory to Mrs Thatcher in 1979, and with it all the oil revenues Labour had gained by extending public ownership in the North Sea, which she sold off to make possible her tax-cuts for the rich.

These facts are never mentioned in the media, because the crisis was used as a golden opportunity to blame the unions and to prepare the way for the wave of privatization which the Tories introduced and which the unions opposed most vigorously. Most people in Britain now share this opposition to privatization, showing how wise the unions were.

The government is now planning further privatization, justifying it on the grounds that it is the only way to find the money needed to improve services, while simultaneously protecting the richest people from any increase in tax at the top rate.

At last, the unions are beginning to sound serious about this new Thatcherite agenda. The GMB has announced a big cut in its donations to the Millbank Tower, so as to release the money saved for its own campaign for public services, publicly owned and publicly accountable. This is undoubtedly the right course for the affiliated unions to take, retaining their subscriptions to the party but converting themselves into active campaigners on behalf of what the Labour movement has always stood for – public services

With the rapid change in public opinion in support of these services, the unions have assumed a major political role, and they can rely on public support for their campaigns.

It has even been suggested that the unions might wish to interview Labour candidates for the forthcoming local government elections to seek their support for public services and opposition to the privatization of local government functions. However, it has not been made clear whether they might go even further and give electoral backing to those non-Labour candidates who share their views, where the official Labour candidates have failed to indicate their support.

These developments should be understood as a serious warning to those at the Millbank Tower who seem to believe that they have a God-given right to force everyone in parliament or on a local authority to vote unthinkingly for whatever the New Labour leadership wants.

The handling of the rail disputes is another case in point. Rumours are circulating that ministers may even be thinking of banning strikes in the public sector – a policy pursued by both Mussolini and Hitler and one which is quite incompatible with New Labour's much-proclaimed view that government should keep out of industrial matters. (This argument has been used to justify governmental inactivity, when private companies shed thousands of jobs after having made a complete mess of their businesses.)

The Labour Party was set up by the unions to protect working people; it was not set up to join with the bosses in their efforts to control labour so as to maximize their profits.

If New Labour were to take a conscious decision to break with the unions it would be the end of its prospects of re-election.

18 January 2002

A warning from history

In 1931, during the world economic crisis, the bankers ordered the then Labour government to make massive cuts in public expenditure to restore 'stability'. The Cabinet met several times to decide how to respond, but the Prime Minister, Ramsay MacDonald, who, along with Keir Hardie, was one of the founders of the Labour Party, believed that he had no alternative but to capitulate to this pressure. He tried to get his colleagues to agree, but some of them refused to go along with it.

MacDonald asked the National Executive of the Labour Party if they would support him, and the NEC told him that they would go along with whatever he recommended, but the TUC flatly refused and indicated that if he did make the cuts they would come out against him.

He had, however, been secretly negotiating with the Tories and the Liberals to enter into a coalition in order to make the cuts and carry them through the Commons. He then himself resigned as the Labour Prime Minister, but was immediately re-appointed as the head of this new National Government which called for the dissolution of parliament to pave the way for a general election against the opposition of the Labour Party.

The Cabinet minutes for the period have long been released under the 30-year rule, and they describe exactly how this situation developed, covering both the end of the Labour government and the first meeting of the new National Government, also under Ramsay MacDonald, which record the congratulations which he received from his Tory and Liberal colleagues.

MacDonald fought that election against the party he had worked to found. He virtually wiped it out, with only 51 Labour MPs left in parliament, yet he stayed at No. 10 for a further four years, and two more after that as Lord President of the Council under Stanley Baldwin.

During that election campaign, in which all the affiliated unions stayed loyal to Labour, Philip Snowden, the Chancellor of the Exchequer, who defected with Ramsay, described the Labour Party as 'Bolshevism run mad', and thus used the Red scare against his old comrades who had placed their faith in him.

For the next fourteen years Labour was in opposition, gaining a hundred more seats in 1935 and then, ten years later, winning a landslide victory which gave us the Welfare State, full employment, full trade union rights and the National Health Service.

Reading this week of the attack on those who want the public services to be publicly funded, publicly owned and publicly accountable as 'Wreckers' brought back these memories. It was almost as if the trade unions representing public-sector workers were being accused of favouring 'Bolshevism run mad' and as if some ministers were implying that the Tories, which introduced privatization under Mrs Thatcher, were their natural allies in following business-friendly policies.

I have never heard the bosses of Railtrack, Enron or Marconi, who have failed so miserably, described by ministers, as 'wreckers', though that charge might well have been made and those who worked for the companies concerned are bitterly resentful at the way they have been treated.

The Prime Minister once said that 'New Labour is a new political party'. So much of what it does and says confirms that view and awakens in me a deep fear that history may be repeating itself on the 1931 model, leaving Labour fatally damaged in the eyes of the electors but the Prime Minister safe in Downing Street with support from Tories and Liberals.

Some on the Left use this argument to justify their decision to leave the party, arguing that it has gone beyond recall and now that its own internal democracy has been virtually destroyed it can never recover. However, those who say that are forgetting the other part of the story: namely that in 1931 it was the trade unions that saved the party and re-equipped it for its later victories.

That process is already under way again with the brilliant advertising campaigns now being launched by the unions in support of the public services. These are now winning widespread popular support from those who depend on them, so wide in fact that even the *Mail on Sunday* has announced that it intends to argue for the Post Office to be retained as a public service.

I walked from my home to Transport House to join the Labour Party on my birthday, sixty years ago this April. I intend to die in the party – though not quite yet – but I never joined New Labour and have no intention whatever of doing so. Indeed, if it goes on like this, it might prove to be too right-wing to be electable.

The Left will never be able to agree on a common ideological position, because socialism, like many other faiths, positively breeds sectarian differences. However, at least we can all work together for jobs, peace and freedom, whatever party we are in, and the campaigns on globalization, privatization, pensions and the war have brought us all together in a way that respects our differences but emphasizes our common aims.

The story of the betrayal of 1931, now over 70 years ago, may seem remote to many readers of the *Morning Star*, but I personally shall never forget it, because in 1930, as a five-year-old, I met MacDonald, when he still was the Labour Prime Minister. He gave me a chocolate biscuit, so I have been a bit suspicious of all Labour leaders with chocolate biscuits ever since – and there are quite a few about now – but no one in the trade union movement seems to be tempted, and we are staying loyal to the real Labour Party.

8 February 2002

A workers' charter

The victory of Jean-Marie Le Pen against Lionel Jospin in the first round of the French elections has given an even greater importance to Saturday's lunchtime rally for a workers' charter at the Friends' Meeting House in London.

For what is now clear is that the policies of the Third Way as practised by New Labour could well lead to a renaissance of the hard Right in Europe, and even in Britain too, unless the trade unions now take the lead and rescue the Labour Party from the grip of big business, Bush and Berlusconi.

For the immediate and most obvious effect of the policies now being pursued is that millions of people feel unrepresented and their concerns ignored, so that some of them take refuge in blaming asylum-seekers and immigrants instead of seeing it as the direct result of capitalism here and world-wide.

Others on the Left in Britain, inside and outside the Labour Party, have long seen and understood exactly what is happening, and the anti-globalization movement has been organized both to explain it and also to resist it, winning very widespread backing from young people, the peace movement, environmentalists and some church people. Millions more across the world are a part of that same campaign.

But the key to success lies with the unions, which are being radicalized by the obvious hostility they are experiencing in their dealings with the government. This is highlighted by the Prime Minister's comparison of his proposed changes in the public services with what Thatcher did to the unions in the 1980s.

When, after 1997, it became clear that the anti-trade union laws were not to be repealed, warning lights started to flash. Our labour laws are now the harshest in Europe, in order to attract investment by promising protection for companies if they come to this country.

The movement to 'Reclaim our Rights', in which John Hendy has played such a significant role, has thus become the trigger for a far bigger campaign to reclaim the Labour Party itself from a small right-wing clique who seized it in a *coup d'état*, claiming that only New Labour could ever defeat the Tories.

But the rejection of Lionel Jospin and the French socialists, who began well but drifted to the right, should alert us to the possibility that New Labour too might actually pave the way for a swing to the right here.

So in the campaign to win back the hard-fought rights of working people which we lost under the Tories our agenda needs to be far bolder, its sights raised higher and its focus made clearer, for what is at stake requires it.

This poses a serious problem for those on the Left who have to decide where to put their main effort and what political formations they should support. This is not easy, as there are now quite a few socialist parties planning to contest the next election, some basing their appeal on the failure of the government.

Each individual has to make his or her own decision on

polling day, but it is worth noting the fact that if all the parties of the Left in France had been united they might well have defeated Le Pen and ended up in a race with Chirac which they could even have won, since Jospin's own supporters might well have backed them in the second round.

Tomorrow at the Friends' Meeting House all these issues will need to be discussed, and with eleven general secretaries of major unions speaking on the platform this will be representative of millions of workers who feel let down, shut out and made scapegoats for the failings of capitalism.

Every campaign we plan must be positive and constructive in its objectives and reassuring to those whom it is intended to help, for the right-wing press will be ready to echo all the warnings about wreckers which Margaret Thatcher used and which are still coming from No. 10, in the hope of rebuilding the Tory victories of 1979 and later.

The socialist historian, R. H. Tawney once said that if fascism came to Britain it would come in a top-hat, and now I know exactly what he meant, for present policies do have some resonance with the days of Mussolini's Italy.

Mussolini was a socialist before the First World War. His swing to the hard Right allowed him to retain a certain credibility with Italian workers which he used to destroy democracy and build a powerful state machine (funded by big business). This made him a hero of the Right in Britain and a natural ally of Hitler's far more brutal Nazi movement.

If the world economy were to go into a recession, as could happen, and if Britain gets sucked into a war with Iraq that could send the Middle East up in flames, as seems very likely, the forces of the Right here could become much stronger, identifying all Muslims, socialists and trade unionists together with those who are opposed to globalization as enemies of the people who must be destroyed.

But none of this need happen, and tomorrow we shall have to make it clear that we will not let it happen. We will mobilize the full strength of our movement, bringing together black and white, women and men in a formidable alliance for peace, justice and freedom, just as the socialist pioneers did in the nineteenth and twentieth centuries.

When they started they did not know if it could succeed, and we must study their experience and see that this time it does.

26 April 2002

Local government

Most of the media coverage of last week's local elections concentrated on turnout, the British National Party (BNP) and a couple of unexpected results in the election for mayor which made the headlines. However, the real issue about the future of local government hardly merited any serious comment, yet that is the problem that has to be tackled if we are to have effective democratic control of the communities in which we live.

'Gas and water socialism', as it was known, once flourished. Councils provided a wide range of services which people really needed, including municipal hospitals, schools, bus services, electricity and houses (essential for millions of residents who could not afford to buy them).

After the last war, over 300,000 houses a year were built to replace those destroyed by bombing and the old slums which disfigured our towns and denied so many families the opportunity to live in dignity and have the space necessary to bring up their children. Some moved to pre-fabs, which were quite popular at the time; others to tower-blocks, which were not; and most to really good homes, well-designed and well-constructed.

As an MP doing my weekly surgeries, many of the problems brought to me related to housing and, although the waiting-lists got longer, the housing manager was usually able to respond quite quickly to an urgent appeal for help, that is until the sale of council houses reduced the stock at the disposal of the council.

A right to buy for everyone sounded so attractive. Councils had always been ready to consider applications to buy, even before the new policy came in, but were required to take account of local need before doing so. Suddenly, available stock fell and replacement building came to a virtual standstill, except for old people's bunga-lows. Those who took out a mortgage to buy became home-buyers and not really home-owners. Now – to add insult to injury – some who did buy have discovered that they may have to sell their houses to pay the cost of care in old age, which is outrageous.

Councils were once assured by Labour that the money raised when they sold their houses would be available to build new ones. They were then told that the money must go on repairs, and now this government is positively encouraging them to hold referenda to authorize the transfer of the whole of their council housing to housing associations, which are exempt from democratic control.

This is the most blatant example of neo-privatization. Some tenants have gone along with it on the grounds that these associations are supposed to be non-profit-making and have an obligation to provide for affordable housing to be included in their development plans. However, in Birmingham a scheme of this kind was recently defeated, which indicates that enough people knew what it was really about and voted accordingly.

In London, where massive new high-cost luxury apartments are going up all over the place, house prices are rising at an astronomic rate. One housing association has been told that the definition of an affordable house is one priced at below £200,000, which is far beyond what a young teacher or nurse, or low-paid worker can possibly afford. This may explain why we cannot recruit the staff we need for the NHS or our schools.

Councils should be able to build enough houses to meet their local needs, and indeed to undertake any project which is, in their opinion, necessary for the community they serve, borrowing at a preferential rate for that purpose, as once used to happen. All the restrictions placed on them by the Tories, and unwisely retained by this government, should be scrapped.

If that were done, the vitality of local democracy would be restored and local people would feel that they were being represented and not (as now) managed by local councillors on behalf of the Treasury. (The latter would like to control every last penny spent and keep the total down to the minimum to satisfy the bankers in Frankfurt who, under the Maastricht Treaty, supervise our economy without having been elected by anybody.)

Until we liberate local authorities to do the job that

people expect of them, we should not be surprised to find that crank candidates get elected, and that many who ought to vote do not do so, out of cynicism or despair. That is the opening that the BNP have been waiting for, in order to exploit local grievances by blaming asylum-seekers, many of whom are themselves just as much victims of global capitalism as those who persecute them.

Having local mayors invested with huge executive powers will also reduce their accountability to those they serve, and could even open the way to corruption, as in America where some councils only meet once a year to allocate contracts and have little else to do.

And this is where privatization comes in at the local level. Councils are being forced to put out more work to tender, allowing private firms to employ staff at lower wages and with poorer conditions. These firms can undercut in-house bids, which leads to redundancies among experienced and committed public servants who know the job and do it conscientiously and well.

It is absurd to argue for devolution and at the same time to keep local councils restricted by law in what they are allowed to do, while private businesses can do anything provided it is not illegal. If Ministers really believe in local democracy the remedy lies with them.

Gas and water socialism, and more, could be the best way to boost election turnout, end cynicism and keep out the cranks and racists who otherwise may creep in by the back-door.

10 May 2002

Giving Labour a voice

The new legislation affecting cross-media ownership has been widely discussed in the press and will be argued over in detail when parliament debates the bill because of the possibility that foreign companies may take over more of our domestic services and monopolies will increasingly dominate the outlets here. These organizations are already very powerful and have a huge influence in shaping our thinking. They now stand to become even more powerful.

This trend, combined with the systematic dumbing down of the programmes we see on our screens, and the ongoing impact of tabloid journalism – all justified by reference to market forces – are creating a political force far greater than any democratic pressures for justice, which have been so widely ignored or dismissed, and even more powerful than parliament itself.

No better example of this can be found than in the way trade unionism has been marginalized in the media, to the extent that its work is very largely ignored except when industrial action is imminent. Then we hear ritual denunciations of extremism in every bulletin, reinforced by solemn and pompous leading articles by editors who never move outside the golden triangle of Westminster, Whitehall and the City of London.

These attacks all began many years ago when the establishment woke up to the fact that the trade unions were strong and growing. They had acquired, through their link with the Labour Party – which they set up to represent them in parliament – a real political influence on government policy. Thus we gained the Welfare State and the NHS, all funded by the necessary levels of redistributive taxation, and limiting the scope for commercial owner-ship of those public services which, in private hands, would have put the search for profit above the needs of those whom the services were designed to serve.

Union officials began to be described as 'bosses' and the leaders were dubbed the 'barons' of the TUC, con-veniently overlooking the fact that real bosses and barons are not elected, unlike general secretaries. If they defended wages or working conditions unionists were described as 'wreckers' and 'trouble-makers' who were trying to run the country.

In my own long life in politics I have never known a single period when the trade unions ran the country or the general secretaries had even a fraction of the power exer-cised by business leaders, especially those multinational corporations which now bestraddle the world and feel free to dictate to governments, as happens regularly.

Now we are seeing this power extended by the growing practice of huge business contributions to New Labour. Such contributions are given without any legal require-ment for a ballot of shareholders of a kind required by law before a union can set up a political fund which even allows individual members to contract out if they wish to do so – a right not extended to shareholders.

Since the passing of Tory anti-union laws – never fully repealed by New Labour – trade unions are threatened by legislation which restricts their rights. For instance, a union taking industrial action which closes a plant, even if only for a day, without a ballot of members, is liable to be fined, but no such action has ever been taken to restrict the right of an employer to close a factory forever, for any reason whatever (and in some cases because it is more profitable to relocate in the Third World where wages are lower).

These laws have made effective trade union action virtually illegal. The media both helped to create the political atmosphere which made this possible and since then have taken the decision to remove almost all references to the trade unions from their programmes. We are hourly bombarded by bankers, stock-brokers, consultants and business advisers who are invited to broadcast every day to air their opinions on everything that happens, while the voice of the unions has been effectively silenced.

Thus union opposition to Tory rail privatization was dismissed as being old-fashioned, yet now almost everyone would like to see the railways brought back into the public sector. Union warnings on rail safety, unheeded at the time, have turned out to be correct.

Union membership, which fell during the Tory years, is beginning to rise again. There are now seven million members, by far the largest voluntary organization in Britain, with a presence in almost all the companies and services in Britain. However, their work in assisting their members is still largely ignored by the mainstream media.

The time has come when a high-level TUC delegation should ask to see the board of governors of the BBC and the Independent Television Commission to demand the introduction of programmes which cover the work they do, on a daily basis, and that leading trade unionists be given the same opportunities to comment on public affairs as are given to business leaders.

Like readers of the *Morning Star*, everyone should have the same access to the work of trade unions, comparable to the business news, so that we can learn about wage settlements, progress made on health and safety, hours of work, unemployment levels and pensions. We should be able to hear special programmes on the prospects for manufacturing industry, education and training, which concern every man and woman in Britain.

If that happened, people would be able to see for themselves what work the unions do and how vital they are to the community. Those who are now disillusioned by the practice of politics might be reassured that they are being represented and would understand why the Labour Party should listen to them.

17 May 2002

Arthur Scargill

This week Arthur Scargill, one of the finest trade union leaders of our generation, retired after a lifetime of service to the National Union of Mineworkers, to the Labour movement and to the ideals of socialism. No man did more than Arthur to defend his members and their families and the communities in which they lived, to protect the environment or to argue for a rational energy policy that took account of the key role that coal should play in the future economy of this country. For all that we owe him a debt of gratitude.

Having known and worked closely with Arthur over a span of nearly 30 years and enjoyed his friendship, I believe that it is important that we should understand and appreciate what he has done, the truth of what he said and what we lost because his warnings were so often disregarded.

No man has suffered more personal vilification than Arthur. He was demonized by the mass media, falsely accused of having behaved improperly – a charge that has been totally disproved – and physically attacked, as when a retired policeman struck him in the stomach with an iron bar in Derby in 1984, when we were speaking together at the May Day rally.

One of the most scandalous incidents took place in the coverage by the BBC of the events at Orgreave, as I learned for myself when I was speaking at a meeting of the National Union of Journalists attended by the BBC TV news team who had prepared the evening bulletin that reported what had happened.

They told me that when the film came in it was clear that the police cavalry had charged the miners before a single stone had been thrown. However, they were told by whoever was in charge to reverse the order of the film to show the stones *being thrown first*, followed by the cavalry charge, thus giving the impression of a riot that the police had to control.

When the Orgreave riot trial came to court, Arthur subpoenaed the police video, which had a time-code on it that confirmed exactly what had happened. Thus the men charged were acquitted.

Mike Figgis, the distinguished producer, has recently made a brilliant film that reconstructs those events, using the men who were there to show exactly what happened. I have seen the film, and I believe it is scheduled to be broadcast later on this year.

Mrs Thatcher decided to destroy the mining industry as a punishment for what she believed the NUM had done to the Tory government in 1974, although, in truth, it was the electors and not the miners who defeated Ted Heath in that general election.

It gave me enormous pleasure that after the 1984–85 miners' strike the Tories threw out Thatcher as Prime Minister and the miners re-elected Scargill as their president, in recognition of his consistency and courage against the fiercest assault ever mounted against any union by any British government.

Arthur was absolutely right in his response to that attack because he knew what the Tory strategy was – to use the defeat of the NUM as a precursor to an even wider attack upon the trade union movement generally with repressive legislation – much of which remains on the statute book five years after a Labour government was elected in 1997.

It is one of the most dangerous myths put out by New Labour, echoing the press proprietors, that it was the resistance of the miners that made Labour unelectable in those years. The truth is the exact opposite, for, if the Labour Party and the TUC had given the NUM the support that it needed Mrs Thatcher would have lost that battle and Labour would have been elected in 1987 – ten years earlier than it was.

Perhaps the greatest disaster for the country as a whole has been the loss of our mining industry and all the brilliant engineering skills of the brave men who worked in very dangerous conditions to give this country the energy it needed for the future. For Britain's industrial revolution was built on coal. Our goods were transported all over the world in coal-fired ships, and the coal reserves we still have today, under our territory, would have lasted a thousand years. (These reserves are now unobtainable, because the industry was destroyed.) Ironically, we are now preparing for another war for Iraqi oil, and this is what President Bush is really interested in.

In reflecting about Arthur Scargill on his retirement, we should also remember his imaginative leadership and his personal courage at the Saltley depot and on many other occasions when he himself actually led and was arrested and victimized.

The women's support groups gave brilliant leadership and inspired many others, including the Women of the Waterfront who backed the Liverpool dockers in their battles and helped many other workers, including those at Wapping when Rupert Murdoch tried to destroy trade unionism there.

Now the tide of public opinion is shifting and it is time that what the NUM, Arthur Scargill, Pete Heathfield, Mick McGahey and their comrades did for us should be recognized. Their struggle still matters for the future, as at some stage we will have to go back to coal.

I wish Arthur Scargill were back with us in the Labour Party, because we need him, but whatever he decides to do we all owe him a big 'thank you' for his work.

2 August 2002

Peace and democracy now

The TUC this week has put democracy back on the political agenda at a time when parliament has been silenced by Downing Street so it can whip up support for the war the White House wants against Iraq – almost as if Britain should act as the propaganda machine for the American Republican Party.

Monday's vote that insisted upon the key role of the UN and the strong opposition expressed to the whole idea of any military attack was the most representative expression of opinion we have had since the present crisis began.

The trade unions are also speaking for most people when they demand an end to privatization, the restoration of full union rights removed by Mrs Thatcher and a return to the earnings link for pensioners – all the more important now that private pensions are under threat.

Who can seriously argue against these policies at a time when privatization has been revealed for what it was – the theft of public assets requiring the taxpayers to pay dividends to shareholders of British Energy when the company itself is bankrupt, like Railtrack which was compensated for its own failure.

The Fire Brigades Union's (FBU) pay claim is unanswerable, and after the display of courage by the American firefighters on September 11, everyone will back them if they take action, all the more sympathetically when they read every day of company fat cats paying themselves huge salaries and vast bonuses.

Indeed, this week at Blackpool we have seen the Labour movement take on its historic role as the champion of democracy, just as it did 200 years ago, when having won its right to organize it threw its weight behind the Chartists who were demanding the vote in a democratic House of Commons to represent them in parliament.

At the end of this month when the Labour conference itself goes to Blackpool it too must express itself with equal clarity and strength. The government will have to listen or risk losing its own claim to speak for those who voted it into power, and public confidence may well melt away.

At this stage the focus must necessarily shift to Labour MPs and Cabinet ministers upon whom the Prime Minister depends for his parliamentary majority and legal right to govern, and credit must be given to those backbenchers who have spoken out so clearly for peace.

Graham Allen's decision to invite MPs to come to London and debate the issues in an unofficial session of the House of Commons – a very imaginative idea – has forced the Prime Minister to recall parliament. This proves that Graham Allen, Tam Dalyell and others were quite right to act as they did, and we shall all benefit.

What we are waiting for now is some clear public statements by senior ministers that they accept the need for decisions by the UN and the Commons before any military action is taken. All we have had up until now have been a few vague hints, passed on informally to 'friends', that some ministers are 'concerned'. This is a gossipy way of trying to win popularity while escaping responsibility for decisions for which they should be accountable.

The more we look at the philosophy of New Labour, the clearer it becomes that it is deeply hostile to democracy itself, believing that market forces, multinational corporations, the WTO, the IMF, the Brussels Commission and the Central Bank in Frankfurt – none of which are elected or can be held accountable – should govern the world.

It is because the British establishment and the City of London know that they can absolutely rely on New

Labour to protect their privileges that they have lost interest in the Tories and see New Labour as the natural heirs of Thatcherism. This is not modernization, but a throwback to the Middle Ages when kings, lords and landowners, backed up by their own armies, controlled the world and were waited on by serfs who had no voice in any of the decisions that affected their lives. If we accept that situation we shall have betrayed all those who won us the liberties we now enjoy.

That is the challenge we have to face, but far from being grounds for discouragement it is our best hope for the future, since the widest support we could hope to win – from across the whole political spectrum – comes when we base our case on democracy, social justice, internationalism and peace.

If we have learned anything from our own history we must know that these objectives can never be obtained by waiting for some new charismatic leader to come and save us, giving us what we want without any effort on our part, for it is movements which make progress and it is to movements that we should give our allegiance.

This is why the TUC, the Labour Party and the peace movement are so important at this moment, and why it is to MPs and not the government that we should be looking for action, encouraging them in every way we can against those who want to hang on to power telling us that 'There is no alternative' or that 'Doing nothing is not an option.'

There is an alternative. War is not the best option, and if we say that loudly enough the message will get through to a world that is yearning for peace.

13 September 2002

7

Miscellany

The Crown versus the people

Now that all the fuss about Sophie Wessex has disappeared from the newspapers, it is a good time for socialists and democrats to look at the importance of the Crown to the British establishment.

This has nothing to do with the royal family, who did not ask for the job but were born in the right beds of the right parents at the right time, or married into the family. There is absolutely no point in attacking individual members of the royal family. This would merely be a diversion from the real question, which centres on how we can establish a genuine democracy in Britain.

The most important role that the Crown performs is to entrench enormous political power which is exercised not by the Monarch but by the Prime Minister of the day. For the Crown prerogatives give the Prime Minister the right to go to war, sign treaties, agree to European laws in Brussels and make a host of public appointments without being required at any stage to seek approval from our elected House of Commons. There was, for instance, no requirement for a parliamentary vote before British troops were sent to war against Iraq or former Yugoslavia because these were all prerogative powers.

Few people realize the role of the Crown in enforcing laws on Britain without the House of Commons ever having voted on them. When a British minister goes to the Council of Ministers in Europe and gives consent to European law, that new European law automatically repeals any existing British laws that conflict with it and creates new laws that no future parliament can repeal.

The power of patronage is also deeply corrupting. The Prime Minister can appoint archbishops and bishops because the Church of England is a state church, and when a bishop is appointed, he has to pay homage by which he declares that he believes in supreme royal power and is opposed to any form of democracy. Similarly, the Prime Minister appoints the judges who then sit as part of the royal courts of justice, designed to maintain the Crown.

The Crown is also the 'fount of honour', and it is by using that fount that the Prime Minister can put people in the House of Lords for life, which gives them the power to delay legislation for at least a year, even when there is a huge Commons majority in favour of it. All the many honours doled out in the honours lists come from above. They are based, not upon what a person who receives them has done but rather on who they were when they did it. Peerages are used to win support for the Prime Minister and sometimes to create vacancies in the House of Commons which the Prime Minister, as a party leader, can then fill through the party machine which may select the short-list and in some cases, actually appoint the candidate for the by-election.

Because we have a hereditary monarch, everyone is brainwashed from birth into believing that they are peculiarly unfitted to pick their head of state, unlike most civilized countries in the world. Every country has always had people who think they are better than everyone else, but Britain is one of the few countries where people are actually taught to think that they are inferior. Top people get the top honours like peerages or knighthoods, but others who have served with great distinction and courage at a lower level in society have to be satisfied with a medal. In the armed forces officers get the Military Cross, while other ranks only get the Military Medal – to hammer home the class basis of the system.

It is no wonder the establishment needs the monarchy and does everything it can to defend itself from its critics, using the argument that to attack the Crown is to attack the royal family but those who believe that the Crown must be maintained at all costs are quite happy to sacrifice individual members of the royal family if by their conduct they endanger the system. For instance, in 1936 the establishment was quite happy to get rid of the king himself, when Edward VIII wanted to marry a divorced American woman, Mrs Simpson, who, it was believed, would weaken the position of the Crown.

For this reason, all the talk about modernizing the monarchy by having stricter rules for members of the royal family and moving the Queen into a more modest home is absolutely irrelevant to the real question.

The time has come when we should begin a serious campaign to elect our head of state and members of our second chamber, and transfer all the royal prerogatives from the Prime Minister to the House of Commons.

Properly presented, this idea could win wide support and be seen for what it is – a long-overdue democratic reform.

18 April 2001

Campaigning for comprehensive education

Speaking in the Oxford Union last month, Chris Woodhead was reported in *The Times* as demanding that comprehensive education should be killed off.

This is the same man who was reappointed by the Labour government in 1997 to continue as Chief Inspector of Schools at OFSTED, and who exercised enormous influence in educational policy until the time when he resigned or was sacked.

During his period in office he seemed to be supported by an alliance of right-wingers, ranging from the Prince of Wales to a senior educational adviser at No. 10, and it was someone else there who coined the phrase 'bog-standard comprehensive', which was a deliberate insult.

As soon as Mr Woodhead was free he launched into a violent attack upon the policy of the government which had employed him, and there is no doubt that he has done a great deal of damage. For not only did he demoralize many teachers by the insensitive, negative and confrontational way in which he conducted his inspections, but it was obvious from the very beginning that he detested the whole idea of comprehensive education, which was designed to give every student access to the whole range of subjects at school.

The arguments used against comprehensive education are usually based upon the totally false claim that they lower standards, playing upon the understandable anxiety of parents that their own children should have the best possible chance at school.

The research of Professor Brian Simon, Professor Clyde Chitty and others has shown conclusively that the so-called 'bright' pupils do as well and the so-called 'average' pupils do much better at comprehensive schools.

In areas where selective education existed, parents of children who 'failed' the eleven plus were the most active in campaigning for comprehensives, which is why so many came into being even during the Thatcher years.

Given all the arguments that support the comprehensive idea it is difficult to escape the conclusion that the case against is in truth based upon a deep hostility on the part of the establishment to the very idea of educating, in the fullest meaning of that word, the working-class.

It is seen as acceptable to allow the 'cleverest' working-class children to go to grammar schools, where they help to raise the average level of attainment when mixed with middle-class children, but the rest must be shunted off into the labour market as soon as possible, trained to obey orders but not to think.

This hostility to the education of the working-class was clearly expressed when the right-wing press conducted its campaigns against what they called the 'Polyocracy' to distinguish those who had gone through 'proper' universities from those who had secured degrees from what had been technical colleges upgraded to university status.

The basis of this critique goes back to the idea that there are different sorts of mind, some intellectual and others more practical, and that to mix them would harm both groups.

In his recent and brilliant inaugural lecture at Goldsmith's College, Professor Clyde Chitty analysed this argument and showed that it stemmed from some of the most reactionary ideas that were based upon the idea that racial purity had to be preserved. Yet, despite all this evidence, we are now slowly slithering back to the idea of selection, through specialist schools, church schools and arbitrary funding, which widens the gap in educational opportunity.

Perhaps the most dangerous development of all is the subtle attempt to downgrade the role of elected LEAs, which alone have the power to eliminate selection, and to move towards the direct funding of individual schools which are able to reintroduce selection at will.

Add to all this government support for the so-called partnership arrangements which bring in private capital and you have the recipe for a throwback to Victorian England when the educational system was deliberately designed to prop up the class system and teach everyone their place in society.

Moreover, in the background there is the General Agreement on Trade in Services which the WTO is trying to impose on us and which would end the democratic control of all our public services by privatizing them all, excluding both parliament and the local authorities altogether. From the point of view of the WTO this would also have the advantage of guaranteeing a system of education, world-wide, where no one was educated to question the power of the multinationals or the WTO or the IMF, but rather would accept that they were slaves serving their masters in the globalized economy.

The problem we face is how to set up a serious discussion about all this, given that the mass media, mainly run by the educationally privileged and owned by the rich and powerful, have no intention of allowing such a debate to take place.

So we have to do it ourselves. Every teacher, educationalist and local councillor who cares should try to organize public meetings in their own area in order to get the debate going, since all our futures depend upon us getting it right.

25 May 2001

From boom to bust – again!

This week it was announced that British manufacturing is officially in recession: 100,000 jobs have been lost this year so far, with another 250,000 at risk. This marks the biggest fall in output for ten years.

Like many children of my generation I vividly remember the chapter in my school history-book which was called 'Britain Becomes the Workshop of the World'. It described the industrial revolution (beginning at the end of the eighteenth century) which made this country strong in technologies that had never before been developed. The British were then the best engineers. They built the factories, pioneered the railways and modern shipbuilding methods, and with a huge mining industry produced the coal which powered the trains and the ships that carried our goods around the world.

The working conditions in Victorian Britain were Dickensian, and in the 'dark satanic mills' which Blake wrote of in his hymn 'Jerusalem', the quality of life was dire. All this gave birth to the trade union movement, the Labour Party and the idea of socialism.

But the level of skill rose to heights never reached before, and although the United States, Germany and Japan caught up and eventually overtook us, that industrial base remained the source of our strength right up until the early 1980s.

Wartime planning was carried over into the period of post-war reconstruction as we nationalized the railways and basic industries such as coal and steel and re-equipped them with new plants for the future, improving health and safety and trade union representation.

In 1945, 48 per cent of all the ships built in the world were launched from British shipyards. In 1970 Britain had the largest motorbike industry in the world. Even as late as 1974 we still had the largest car and machine-tool industries in Europe, and a powerful computer industry too.

When in 1964 Harold Wilson set up the Ministry of Technology, it was to see that manufacturing had the support it needed. He intended the new Department of Energy, ten years later to acquire and use the huge new oil revenues flooding ashore from the North Sea to rebuild our industrial base. But in the twenty years that followed all that was thrown away, deliberately and consciously, by successive governments for reasons that we need to understand.

Mrs Thatcher set out to destroy the trade union movement. She was prepared to pay the price for that by sacrificing our manufacturing base, closing the pits and creating unemployment in order to undermine the unions, selling off the 25 per cent ownership of the North Sea oil which Labour had painfully acquired, as well as privatizing public assets to fund her reactionary policies.

Since New Labour has been in power this country has had no industrial policy at all, apart from working hand-in-glove with multinational corporations and describing all job losses as commercial decisions for which ministers have no responsibility. We are told that we live in a global economy where we have to accept the power of big business. As the Prime Minister said to the TUC in 1999, 'Mass production is out. Go-it-alone macro economics is out. Jobs for life are probably out.'

Having warned us that the Tories were a party of 'boom and bust', it now looks as if the Chancellor has taken a leaf out of their book. Britain is rapidly becoming a Third World country with a big tourist trade, lots of gamblers in the City of London, plenty of industrial museums to tell visitors what we used to produce, a Queen in a palace guarded by toy soldiers and a borrowed Trident from America (which we can keep if we do as they tell us).

If this country is to have a future we must have a flourishing manufacturing industry. This is a basic national interest and it will require an active industrial policy properly funded and supported by any government that wants to be taken seriously.

To do that we need to rebuild our decaying infra-structure, take back our rail system, find the cash needed by our public services (now starved of money by the Treasury) and introduce a fair tax system that is based on social justice instead of ring-fencing the rich to protect them from any tax increases and means-testing the poor.

In short, the ideals that Labour was set up to achieve are back on the political agenda. They have an appeal that goes far beyond the so-called Left, embracing managers and small businesses who also now find themselves struggling to survive.

There will be plenty of opportunities in the next few weeks to put this case at the TUC and Labour Party conferences in Brighton, and ministers would be well advised to listen very carefully indeed. For, if we are indeed heading towards a major world recession then this could lead to a wave of complete disillusionment with all the shallow sound-bite and focus-group language that has characterized the politics of the Millbank Tower.

10 August 2001

Ireland for the Irish

The long-drawn-out discussions that are now taking place about the latest peace proposals from London and Dublin have led to a great deal of mutual recrimination. The blame is attached to either Loyalists or Nationalists, according to the perspective of the person speaking.

Strangely, very little criticism is directed at the British, even though the main cause of the trouble over the centuries can be traced back to the mainland. It is conveniently forgotten that over the centuries every single policy ever pursued by British governments has failed to secure peace in Ireland. Occupation failed, partition failed, Stormont failed, direct ruled failed, as did internment without trial, plastic bullets, CS gas, Diplock courts, supergrass trials, the broadcasting ban, the Prevention of Terrorism Act and the policy of 'shoot to kill' (always denied, but not very convincingly).

During the years when violence was at its height the Loyalists, their Tory friends in parliament and the media always denounced everyone who even tried to talk to Sinn Fein (even though successive governments maintained contact at a high level, but kept it secret). Whenever the IRA suggested a ceasefire it was rejected by the Loyalists on the grounds that there was no guarantee that it would be permanent.

The initiative taken by Tony Blair in 1997, supported by Bill Clinton and followed up by Mo Mowlam as Secretary of State, was the most imaginative and hopeful move ever on the part of a British government. The Belfast Agreement which followed seemed to offer the best chance of finding a political solution that would replace the gun with the ballot-box.

The new assembly and administration, with its North–South links, brought in the Dublin government. Chris Patten issued a report that promised to reform the Royal Ulster Constabulary, seen by the Nationalists as little more than the military arm of Unionism. There was a clear indication that the decommissioning of IRA weapons would be matched by a parallel demilitarization on the part of the British and an end to Loyalist violence.

Whatever David Trimble's real position is – and these things should not be made personal – it is clear that he believes that his continuing leadership of his own party depended upon him issuing an ultimatum, and this is exactly what he has done. But any unbiased observer of the scene knows that the Loyalists bear a heavy responsibility for the deteriorating situation. The annual confrontation over the provocative marches through the Garvachy Road, and this week's horrifying intimidation of young Catholic children on their way to their primary school, helps to explain why a majority of people here in mainland Britain would be glad to see an end to our involvement in Northern Ireland.

It is also obvious that the Loyalist and Nationalist communities have one thing in common – they both distrust the British, though for very different reasons. The Nationalists, wanting Irish unity, have always argued for a British withdrawal to permit Ireland to be governed by the Irish. The Loyalists, despite their loud protestations of attachment to the British Crown and the British state, deeply distrust the Westminster government because they interpret Unionism as giving them the right to continue the old policy of domination of the province, and they resent the peace process for that very reason.

Strangely, the outcome of the Unionist hard line has been that the Irish Republic is now in effect almost an equal partner with a reluctant Britain in governing the North, which cannot have been what Ian Paisley had in mind when he opposed the Belfast Agreement.

It is hard to see how things can now be moved forward, but if the peace process does break down the most likely consequence of it will be not a return to bloodshed, which few want, but a rising demand in Britain for us to withdraw.

The best hope remains for the Good Friday Agreement to be pressed forward by the British government. The agreement reflects the deep desire for peace among all the communities there, but with the most recent examples of Loyalist violence it would be quite wrong for the delay in the decommissioning of weapons by the IRA to be used as an excuse for suspending the peace process.

Peace means the absence of sectarian violence. That is the real test. The policing of the Province must be based on the Patten Report if it is to command the support of both communities, just as the assembly must be retained to give expression to its interests.

The vision of a truly united Ireland, in which peace and cooperation by consent can be achieved, may take time to realize. However, the likelihood of Britain remaining in power in the North for ever is also happily receding, given that most people in Britain do not want this and both sides in Northern Ireland so distrust us.

During this critical interim period those who believe in Ireland for the Irish – as I do – should continue to spell out this aim with clarity, persistence and courage.

7 September 2001

Secrecy is the enemy of democracy

The publication of the 1971 government papers by the Public Record Office tells us a great deal about the discussions that were then going on in the Cabinet about issues that concerned us all. We learn that the Tory government was so anxious to get Britain into the Common Market that nothing was allowed to be said or done which might endanger it, and Ted Heath was determined not to allow the people to have any say in a referendum.

On Northern Ireland we read that the Cabinet even

discussed the possibility of a united Ireland, that the army was opposed to the introduction of internment without trial and that links were being established, however discreetly, with Sinn Fein – at a time when anyone on the Left who was suggesting this was denounced as a friend of terrorism.

We also discover that the plot to undermine and destroy the trade union movement was indeed well-advanced, and the Upper Clyde Shipbuilders were to be the test-case – this having been carefully prepared long beforehand.

If this had all been public knowledge at the time people would have been able to mount much more significant criticisms of what was going on and develop more effective opposition – all of which would have invigorated our democracy.

That, indeed, is why this information is all kept secret by successive governments. They are determined to safeguard themselves from public scrutiny for their own personal and political protection, justifying it on the grounds that it is in the national interest.

A Freedom of Information Act, to which New Labour was committed in the election, has now been quietly deferred because this government, like the Tories 30 years ago, also fears that it would be seriously criticized if the public knew what was really being discussed.

There are in fact very few secrets that really need to be protected (such as the details of military technology, the deployment of forces, emergency defence plans and Britain's negotiating position in advance of an international conference). The rest of what is being kept secret is simply to save ministers from embarrassment.

We shall have to wait for 30 years – until 2031 – before

we are allowed to know what is being discussed in the Cabinet now, at a time when major decisions which affect our lives are being taken leaving us in ignorance of the real arguments.

For example, why cannot we now see the Treasury papers on the euro and the private briefings being given by the Bank of England on the same subject? Why are we denied the assessments being made in Whitehall of the international consequences of a new war on Iraq and other aspects of the policies being pursued by President Bush? Why are we not allowed to know exactly what arguments are going on at the top on the question of rail nationalization and the linking of pensions with earnings?

The answer is simple. It is that if this information was made available the government would find it far harder to win and hold its public support on these and other policies, so it maintains the secrecy and pretends it is all about national security. It almost seems as if parliamentary democracy is only believed to work provided the public can be kept in the dark for a generation until the decisions that were taken have long been forgotten.

The only people with the power to put this right are MPs, who, like the rest of us, are also kept in the dark. However, they do not try to alter the situation because all ministers and shadow ministers are beneficiaries of the system and many backbenchers too are hoping to be ministers or shadow ministers and realize that if they rebelled on this their prospects of promotion would be endangered.

Strangely it was my own experience as a minister that convinced me of the case for open government, because it was the only way to bring in the outside expert advice that a minister needs to reach a decision, unless he is prepared to be satisfied with Civil Service advice. It was, for example, because of the advice that I received from outside Whitehall that I came to see how dangerous and expensive nuclear power was, and that it was really about providing plutonium for the US weapons programme from our so-called peaceful atomic power stations, which were actually bomb factories.

None of this could I have learned any other way. I now believe that far better decisions could be made over a whole range of subjects if ministers were able to draw upon the expertise of others, which would help them to overcome the sense of powerlessness which lies behind so much public disenchantment and electoral apathy.

It would not surprise me if privately some ministers were equally frustrated to find that all the key decisions are being taken in secret by the Prime Minister and a handful of his personal advisers and then imposed on them without hearing what they had to say.

Secret government can never be good government.

2 January 2002

The media and politics

Those on the Left who are actively involved in politics are usually the most critical of the coverage of political issues, and with good reason, for most of the programmes we see and hear are superficial, personalized and underestimate the intelligence of the listener.

There is of course this newspaper and a few honourable exceptions among journalists, people like John Pilger,

Robert Fisk, Paul Foot and Tariq Ali, but the importance of radio and television to the establishment is so great that those who hold a dissenting view are held to be a real threat and their influence has to be limited.

The most vivid examples of the power of the media can be found in the case of Soviet jamming of the BBC years ago, and the bombing of the former Yugoslav TV station in Belgrade during the Kosovo war, which was justified on the grounds that it was playing a key role in the 'enemy' camp.

For the same reason the Al-Jazeera station was detested by the American and British authorities because it allowed another perspective to be broadcast, including comments by Osama bin Laden. Last week the Israelis destroyed a Palestinian radio station in order to silence it.

I have always been interested in the way in which past wars are covered, once the interest of the powers that be have shifted to new events, allowing the broadcasters greater freedom than they had at the time. The exposé of Suez aggression in a recent programme was a good example of that.

No doubt in twenty years time awards at Cannes will go to some bright producer who has made a programme called 'How we got it wrong in the Balkans' or 'The real consequences of the Afghan war', but by then it will be too late to help us to see what was happening when we could have done something about it.

Even so, the very courageous TV documentary on Bloody Sunday that was shown on ITV was well worth watching and has still come in time to allow us to understand why the inquiry into what actually happened is so important for the future in Ireland.

When a good programme on a contemporary issue is put out it becomes far more powerful, as we saw with the brilliant BBC 2 documentary last Sunday 'Correspondent', filmed by Taghi Amirani. He went to visit the Makaki refugee camp and talked to those who were refugees and those who ran the camp, both before and after the Taliban was replaced by the Northern Alliance. What made it so powerful was the objective way in which he conducted the interviews, allowing those to whom he spoke to tell their own stories in their own way. And what awful stories they were: of bombing and deaths and escape from their homes into a desert tent looking for food and clean water.

He made no attempt to construct a political argument, but it would have been unnecessary anyway, for the message came across so clearly. Those who have possibly never thought of it realize how the West ignores the death of innocent people whilst remembering and honouring those killed in New York in September.

If this sort of reporting was developed and encouraged in Britain the whole political scene would change as more and more viewers came to see for themselves the real problems that face so many of their fellow citizens. For example, if instead of broadcasting the business news every hour on the hour, throughout the day and night, showing how the stock markets are moving and highlighting the varying value of the dollar, the pound and the euro, which cannot possibly be of interest to many viewers, the BBC were to put out even daily reports on low wages, unemployment, homelessness, deaths from industrial accidents or asbestosis, the pressure for action would build up at once. No government could afford to disregard it, and would have to act.

Similarly, if we were allowed to hear trade unions get the same coverage as stockbrokers and permitted to talk about their work, problems and achievements it would tilt the balance of argument in industrial affairs, which is not an unreasonable suggestion as there are well over seven million trade unionists, as compared to a few thousand stockbrokers.

Pensioners, environmentalists and many other voluntary organizations, which now only get a chance if there is trouble and then have to face hostile cross-examination from the pundits, should be helped to make their own programmes so we can hear what they are trying to tell us.

The public attitude to politics might even change if the ritualized and synthetic abuse which goes on at Prime Minister's Questions on TV were to be replaced by some of the excellent speeches made by independent back-benchers which we never hear and which the whips in all parties would not want us to hear because they are 'off-message'.

But just by setting out the case for a genuinely free and independent press and broadcasting system explains precisely why the top people would never agree – for they understand what a transformation it would bring about in the political climate of the nation, which is the last thing they want.

Henry VIII nationalized the Church of England because he knew how necessary it was to control the power of the priests. The BBC was nationalized by a Tory government to control the broadcasters, and we have to campaign for a free media even more actively if we want a better system here.

25 January 2002

The Jubilee and democracy

The Jubilee has, as must have been intended, immensely strengthened the existing order and made those at the top feel much more secure in the wealth and privileges which they enjoy, confident that no effective challenge can be mounted against them, at least for the time being.

In that sense the concerts at Buckingham Palace, the parade in the royal coach to St Paul's, the lunch with the Lord Mayor and the fantastically colourful and multi-cultural parade in the Mall have been brilliantly devised and executed to consolidate the idea that the essence of everything British can be best expressed by our common allegiance to a monarch who reigns over us.

In Royal Britain we are expected to confine our loyalty to someone at the top rather than express it in solidarity with our fellow men and women, and this is the basis of the feudal class system within which our duty is to those put above us and to know our place and keep it, out of respect for our betters.

The feudal system is still a very powerful force in Britain, but it has nothing whatever to do with the socialist definition of class which identifies very different economic interests between those who work to create the nation's wealth and the handful at the top who own that wealth.

The perpetual bowing and scraping we have seen over the Jubilee is a celebration of that old class system, whereas the socialist understanding of class was obliterated as symbolized by the absence from the parade of any of the great trade unions which organize the workers. The only reference to the unions was a huge puppet depicting a despondent miner and a cardboard cut-out of Arthur Scargill on a float showing well-known people who have lived while the Queen has been on the throne.

This elimination from our political vocabulary of class, in its socialist sense, has been planned for a long time because when it became a political force with the emergence of the Labour and socialist movement a hundred and more years ago it divided the nation into haves and have-nots, and that analysis looked as if it might destabilize the feudal system for the simple reason that with the arrival of universal adult suffrage it was obvious that the have-nots could – if organized – have outvoted the haves.

That is why the Thatcher government made it its business to destroy, so far as it could, all the structures of working-class power, especially the trade unions and local authorities where Labour was strong. The Tories began the process of dismantling the welfare state and the public services by privatization, summing it all up by announcing as she did that 'There is no such thing as society' and 'There is no alternative' to frighten off those who might challenge her.

Politically the immense legal powers in our monarchy do not lie with the Monarch, but with the Prime Minister of the day, who personally exercises all these Crown prerogatives and does so without the need to get the authority of the elected House of Commons which has no control whatever, and which is not even allowed to vote before Britain goes to war, or agree to new laws imposed by the Council of Ministers in Brussels. The power of patronage, including the grant of peerages and honours, is personal to the Prime Minister too.

This is the gaping democratic hole lying at the very heart of our parliamentary system. It explains why every Prime Minister, Labour and Tory, passionately supports the monarchy – which is necessary to retain those powers – and why the monarch depends on every Prime Minister to provide the political support which the monarchy needs to survive.

So important is the monarchy to the political establishment that they would be quite happy to ditch a king or queen to save the institution, as happened when Edward VIII was forced to abdicate for fear that his marriage to an American divorcee might shake public confidence in the system. The establishment would act similarly if it thought it necessary to do so.

It is, in my opinion, a great mistake for republicans to criticize the Queen herself, because it is the issue and not the individual which should concern us. The Queen did not pick the job. She was born of the right parents, in the right bed at the right time and has for 50 years done all that could have been required of her. This explains the genuine affection that many people feel for her, as has become very clear especially during the last few months and days.

Personally I would have no objection whatever if she continued to call herself queen and live at Buckingham Palace to attract tourists as a privatized and profitable business, so long as we could elect our own first citizen and make him or her fully accountable to the parliament we choose on polling day.

But that is not what the people at the top want and for them the Jubilee has provided a marvellous opportunity to put the clock back more than a hundred years by providing bread and circuses for the peasants and allowing the powerful to celebrate their new-found sense of security.

This is a system which has lasted for far too long, and it should act as a reminder to all democrats and socialists that the Labour movement has got to start building itself up, all over again, if we really believe in self-government and intend to achieve it in Britain.

7 June 2002

Recognition in a democracy

Twice a year the Queen's honours list is published and we are told which rich and famous people are to be made Lords with a seat for life in parliament and who are to become Sir John this or Dame Jane that, in recognition of their supposedly valuable contribution to the nation. To make it all sound a bit more democratic, there are hundreds of other names on the list, including some brave postmistress who has fought off a gang who attacked her and a traffic warden who has served faithfully for 47 years.

Apart from a very few who may get a peerage for marrying a member of the Royal Family or for performing some act of personal service to the sovereign, which are in the personal gift of the Queen, all the names on the list are drawn up by the Prime Minister or ministers with the help of civil servants, but since the Queen, by law, is the fount of all honour, her name goes at the top of the official announcement and some of the top awards are handed out by her at an investiture in Buckingham Palace.

It is obvious that all Prime Ministers will want to

reward their political friends and supporters, attempt to win more friends from amongst those who may not have been so helpful but could possibly be induced to take a more positive view if they have some recognition, and to please the tabloids, and to show how closely the Queen and No. 10 Downing Street are in touch with public feeling, some famous pop star or footballer will probably be included.

When Lloyd George was Prime Minister he actually sold honours for cash and used the money for his personal political fundraising, but then corruption and honours have always gone hand in hand from the very beginning. Indeed, some believe that the two are virtually indivisible by the very nature of the patronage process.

The less glamorous honours are put to ministers to approve by civil servants in their own departments and will normally go through on the nod, but even at the lower level the patronage system still works. I recall one permanent secretary, who had recommended a knighthood for a particular industrialist, being given a directorship in that man's company when he himself retired from the Civil Service a year or two later.

But apart from the sniff of traditional sleaze, which has always surrounded the system, what is wrong with it is that all honours come from the top and none have any democratic legitimacy about them. The awards given relate to the social class of the recipient and not the service that has been rendered.

The top brass in Whitehall and the City are the ones who get the peerages and the knighthoods, and our sub-postmistress may get a medal at the lowest level and will not be asked to an investiture to receive it. If she can be persuaded that it really is the Queen's personal wish that she should have it then she may become a passionate supporter of the monarchy, the class system and the status quo – which is what the Jubilee was all about.

Contrast this way of saying thank you with the more democratic procedures that do exist, as for example when a university votes to award some distinguished scientist an honorary degree, or a city votes to make a citizen a Freeman of the Borough, both of which carry with them the authority of a collective decision without any fount of honour having gushed forth upon the grateful recipient.

It is the same when a trade union gives someone life membership after that member has devoted himself or herself to the work of that union, or even honours some person outside the union who is deemed to have made a genuine contribution to the cause.

It would be perfectly possible – and extremely desirable – for the House of Commons to take over the honours system from the Prime Minister by inviting nominations from MPs, local authorities and other public bodies, which together with the citations would be published in a motion of thanks which could be formally debated and passed, followed by a reception for those named, all of whom would be given their own citation, suitably framed and a single medal struck to mark their award.

In this way the whole system would be democratic, freed from all personal patronage and genuinely open at every stage to allow those who really have performed a service to feel that they had been recognized. This would encourage all the people who do a good job, especially in the public services where financial rewards are well below those in private industry.

Encouragement is a much more effective way of getting results than the practice of naming and shaming adopted by OFSTED in their dealing with schools that were struggling against difficult circumstances to help the students in their care. The passion for grading everyone and publishing league tables has had a similarly depressing effect, just as the eleven plus examinations did before comprehensives came in to end the classification of children as failures so early in their school careers.

It has long seemed to me that there are those who positively dislike the idea that working-class children should get a better education because it might lead to them asking awkward questions about the society in which they live and it would be better if they were just trained to take orders and know their place in society so that the class system can continue unchallenged.

That is also what the present honours list is all about. Speaking for myself, I would far rather be an honorary member of the NUM, as indeed I am – membership no. 001 – than be in the House of Lords. I don't have to prove it!

21 June 2002

The case for liberating the Church

The Synod of the Church of England voted this week to retain the system by which the Prime Minister appoints all the bishops and archbishops, in the name of the Queen, making it the only church in the Anglican communion world-wide which is nationalized, since the Church of Wales was disestablished in the 1920s and the Scottish Episcopalian Church makes its own appointments.

It all began in 1533, when the Henry VIII felt threatened by the Pope, having discovered the latter was raising more money in taxation than he was, so he took it over and it has been a state church ever since.

From the King's point of view this was a brilliant move because it allowed him to put a priest in every pulpit, in every parish, every Sunday, telling the faithful that God wanted them to do what the King wanted them to do, and the Church was then the mass media and was kept under tight royal control.

The King appointed the bishops and the archbishops, and even today every bishop on appointment has to swear homage to the Crown, using the following words: 'I do hereby declare that Your Majesty is the only supreme governor of this your realm, in spiritual and ecclesiastical things as well as in temporal', so that to become a bishop you have to deny the legitimacy of democracy and are rewarded with a seat in the House of Lords.

Nowadays all royal prerogatives are exercised by the Prime Minister and, when there is a vacancy, a committee, representing the Church, puts forward two names and the Prime Minister chooses the one he or she wants – or can even ask for further names – despite the fact that, by law, the Prime Minister is not required to be a member of the Church of England, or even a Christian, and could indeed be a Catholic, Methodist, Jew, Muslim or atheist.

If any Prime Minister were to announce today that he intended to nationalize the Roman Catholic Church, the Methodists, Baptists or Congregationalists, take over the synagogues or mosques and appoint the rabbis, mullahs and imams the idea would universally denounced because it would completely destroy the independence of those religions and their ability to criticize the government on moral grounds, which is exactly the problem facing the established Church of England.

That the Synod voted to keep this system unchanged tells us a lot about how undemocratic Britain is, which is why the Prime Minister must be delighted because he appoints the ministers in his government, members of the House of Lords and the Chairman of the Labour Party (who used to be elected). He knows that any ambitious young priest, who might hope one day to become a bishop, will never dare to criticize his government.

The Queen also likes it because, to make up for the fact that she is not elected, the Archbishop of Canterbury, at her coronation, speaks of her as God's choice for the throne.

It also means that when there is a war in which British troops are involved, Anglican chaplains will bless the soldiers as they go to battle, and by describing it as a 'Just War', use God's name to legitimize the killing of those innocent civilians who become victims of the bombing of their towns and villages.

The Church likes it because the bishops sit in the House of Lords and, without being elected, decide upon the laws we are expected to follow. They enjoy a privileged position in our society and it can be argued that these privileges make this a Christian country, without the need to preach and convert people to accept the message of Jesus and make it relevant to their lives.

Religion, Marx said, is the 'opium of the people'. He must have been referring to the way that the Church is used to prop up the existing order and keep the working-class in their place as loyal subjects of the Queen and obedient serfs in modern feudal society, where the multi-nationals have taken over from the old landlords and exploit us for their own profit.

The role of religious leaders as teachers, alerting us to the moral factors in decision-making, preaching brotherhood, internationalism and peace is very important, and indeed the socialist faith owes much to Christian teaching because it has encouraged people to believe that if we are all equal in the eyes of God we ought to enjoy that equality in our political and economic lives as well.

Many devout people have been ready to die for their faith, just as socialists have been, but historically we know that, on other occasions, religious leaders tell people to kill for their doctrine, and that is a threat to the survival of the human race.

So when the Synod voted to keep the Church as a part of the state machine, they abandoned their responsibilities as religious teachers and chose to kneel before the Queen, the government and those who own the wealth that buys them the privileges the bishops want to share in the House of Lords.

The Bible tells many stories about kings who had power and prophets who preached righteousness and often challenged the kings in what they did. In modern Britain, however, the kings appoint the prophets and in this way obliterate the prophetic message that we desperately need if the human race is to survive in this dangerous world. It is worth noting that many good Christians reject the whole idea that the state should control their church.

Indeed, if we are ever to get peace in the world all religious leaders should aim to free themselves from nationalism and jointly excavate the foundations of all faiths, which are rooted in a commitment to preserve all life on this earth by encouraging good and discouraging evil – a message that has a particular relevance today.

12 July 2002

Here is the news

Every hour the BBC and ITV give us an update on the business news, with movements of the Dow Jones and the Footsie, together with information on the fluctuations between the value of the dollar, the euro and the pound sterling. This is always explained to us as if it was the main interest of the viewers, presumably to help pensioners rush out to sell their dollars and buy euros while the rate is favourable.

Those who wake really early can watch a full half-hour before 6 a.m. on the BBC when financial correspondents in Wall Street and elsewhere report on individual share prices of the major corporations. They do so with all the gravity you would expect of a commentary on a service in a cathedral, which in a sense it is, since all this information is part of an ongoing act of worship for those who see money as their god.

I would be very surprised if those who work in the City of London rely on this to guide them in their own decisions, because they are all fully equipped with lap-tops, mobile phones, fax machines and pagers that keep them posted on a minute-by-minute basis. And they are probably far too busy gambling with millions to turn on their television sets.

That is one definition of news, but for those who are interested in politics we have a regular diet of lobby correspondents who stand outside No. 10 Downing Street to keep us fully informed about the prospects for a Cabinet reshuffle, or an update on the argument between Black Rod and the Prime Minister about exactly where he stood during the Queen Mother's funeral and which frontbencher is expected to come out of the closet within the next few days.

Then there are regular photo opportunities to show one minister reading a book to some schoolchildren, another dressed in a white coat leaning over a patient in a hospital that has been built under the private finance initiative and a tough briefing from the Ministry of Defence to explain how the Pentagon in Washington absolutely depend upon British bombers to carry through their operation to remove Saddam Hussein (even though we have been assured that no decision has been made on whether to go to war).

To help us to understand all this the media have a battery of academic experts on call, who can fill in the background with a few statistics. These are then further explored by getting a round table of pollsters and political pundits who can be relied upon to assess the political significance for the party leaders and dismiss a few maverick MPs and agitators whom, we are assured, can be safely disregarded as having no influence in their own parties.

When Michael Meacher courageously and correctly indicated this week that he felt that he was a lone voice in the wilderness arguing that the environment was not taken seriously by the government he was shining a welcome shaft of light on the world of spin, helping us to see through it all. Predictably, however, his comments were immediately brushed aside by an unidentified spokesman from No. 10 whose job it is to see that no real debate on the issue was to be allowed.

The environment is a subject that is really too hot to handle because it poses a threat to those multinationals that make some of their profit by despoiling the planet. Dedicated Green campaigners can then be reclassified as ecoterrorists and dealt with under the new legislation passed to deal with the threat posed by Osama bin Laden on September 11.

The real opium of the people today is no longer religion but the extensive coverage of sport, the silly game-shows, confession and synthetic confrontation programmes which encourage people to tell all and 'Big Brother', which encourages us to hope that we shall see all. These are interspersed with films spattered with violence and sex that must explain the behaviour of those for whom killing apparently seems quite normal.

The Director-General of the BBC, who has been pushing through the digital revolution, has reassured us that BBC 4 is for those who want to think. This leaves people like me, who still only have BBC 1 and BBC 2, with apparently no legitimate reason to believe that they will encouraged to think by either of those mainstream outlets.

Meanwhile life goes on outside this closed circle, and no one knows it better than the trade union movement whose interests and activities are systematically ignored unless there is some form of industrial action, in which case the BBC will revert to its old language and talk about the 'barons' and 'bosses' of the trade unions holding the country to ransom. (Funnily enough, neither the real barons who sit in the House of Lords or the real bosses who run big business have ever been elected by those they lead, as happens in all trade unions.)

But lest all this leads anyone to despair, let us note and remember the clear signs that neglect of important issues by those at the top do not prevent them from surfacing. We have seen this with the anti-war movement, which was dismissed a few months ago as a typical minority of troublemakers and now commands the support of the new Archbishop of Canterbury and a majority of the citizens of this country.

It is such a pity that when people move to bring about progress they get so little coverage or help from those who run our media, but determination and commitment in a good cause can prosper and the only real losers are those who think they know everything but actually know a lot less about what is going on than readers of the *Morning Star*.

16 August 2002

Right and wrong

The other day, I heard some pundit on the radio say, almost casually, that there was now no difference between Left and Right in British politics, as if that automatically disposed, without further argument, of the critique that socialists have always made of capitalism and the validity of the socialist case.

The fact that such a statement could be made, and remain unchallenged, proved the success of the long establishment campaign to eliminate socialist ideas from our political analysis and vocabulary, with the effect that many people have actually been persuaded that everyone is middle-class and only the lazy and incompetent ever become poor, unemployed or homeless.

Similarly we are assured by the financial commentators that the fat cats with their massive pay-offs deserve every penny they get by virtue of their hard work and entrepreneurial skills, even if they made it by gambling with money that others have earned or by insider trading that is a form of theft.

The same analysis holds sway world-wide, with the American dream held up as the one to which we should all aspire, and poverty in the Third World being attributed to corrupt governments and tribal wars – as if the West never experienced any comparable problems.

In this way those in power hope to remove any possible challenge to their privileges by suggesting that the criteria used to justify their actions are validated by the profitability test: if a project can be shown to be unprofitable we are all expected to oppose it without question. Of course all wars are unprofitable, but they are held to be beyond the profit test. Having said that, of course wars are intensely profitable for arms manufacturers, while the taxpayers pay because it is their national duty.

There are other arguments, besides profit, that are put forward to secure compliance with policies that few people would ever accept. For example, there are arguments based upon populist patriotism, now being used in the United States, to justify not only the war preparations but also the conscious abandonment of many long-cherished civil liberties supposedly to fight terrorism.

Those in Britain who may dare to disagree with the Prime Minister and New Labour are told that they are being disloyal to the leader or unhelpful in their criticisms of the government, or that they are making impossible demands that are unrealistic for the party. And ministers, advised by their spin-doctors, may recommend that the government itself should abandon policies, even good ones, solely because they may be unpopular with the media proprietors who can influence the electors against them.

Then we are also warned that some actions cannot be sanctioned because they are illegal, as in relation to the anti-trade union laws introduced by the Tories and never repealed, diktats imposed by the bankers in Frankfurt, the bureaucrats in Brussels, or the multinationals which bring their pressure to bear through the WTO and the IMF.

And those who take direct action, like the Greenham Common women, can be hauled up before the courts and punished for what they have done, even though history will reverse that judgement, as with the Tolpuddle Martyrs, conscientious objectors, or the suffragettes (who were imprisoned under unjust man-made laws that should never have been passed and which should be repealed).

All these arguments that socialist ideas are unprofitable, unpatriotic, disloyal, unrealistic, unpopular or illegal have been invented to silence us and persuade us take orders from those who now have power and arrogantly claim, by virtue of their knowledge and expertise, to know better than we do.

This is the thinking that lies behind the assertion that there is now no difference between Right and Left, but what about the much more important argument that always goes on between what is Right and what is Wrong – the moral argument that raises really awkward questions that anyone can ask of those at the top, even if they do not have a degree in business studies or any technical expertise?

I was brought up on the Bible by my mother who told me about the age-old conflict between the kings who had power and the prophets who preached righteousness. She taught me to support the prophets against the kings, meaning that each of us had the responsibility for learning to differentiate between good and evil and make that our guide for action.

She was right, we should all have the confidence to think things out for ourselves, and if we do it must be clear that Bush's plan to make war on Iraq is wrong, as is the conduct of Sharon in oppressing the Palestinians, or the whipping up of hostility against asylum-seekers, or accepting the present grossly unfair division between rich and poor in a world dominated by globalization.

To reintroduce the criteria of Right and Wrong into our political debates would not necessarily make it easier to resolve arguments or reach agreement, but at least we would all be arguing on a basis that everyone could understand and where each of us could claim the same moral right to hold a view and have it heard, respected and given equal weight.

Were such a revolutionary idea ever to be accepted you can be sure that the rich and powerful would be outvoted all the time because capitalism shields behind their own phoney criteria and fears. The strength of the socialist case is that it is based upon morality, which is why we should have the courage to argue for it boldly, clearly and confidently.

23 August 2002

America under Bush

Within a few weeks the American nation will be going to the polls for the mid-term Congressional elections, and at about the same time it will be launching a massive military attack on Iraq, using the most powerful weapons of mass destruction that exist anywhere in the world.

In those elections Bush is playing the patriotic card, trying to win votes, as many leaders have done throughout history, by being the strong man against some foreign enemy. It may work, as Mrs Thatcher proved in 1983 after the Falklands war – which was also about oil.

Both Bush and Thatcher hoped that the people could be diverted from the failure of their domestic policies, relying on the mass media to focus everyone's attention on the grand imperial adventure upon which they were engaged. But although the problems facing the American people may not be highlighted in the media, here or there, they still exist and cause justifiable anxiety for those many millions who face them in their daily lives.

I am lucky not to have to rely on the press to tell me what is happening in the United States because a brilliant website which calls itself PORTSIDE (*portsidemod@yahoo.com*) send me e-mails every day. This week I read about the real situation, all derived from published sources, many of them official publications issued by the American government and compiled by Congressman Henry Waxman from California.

I pass them on because they tell you a lot about Mr Blair's new-found ally Mr Bush, who also believes passionately in the value of market forces as the surest way to modernize society and become a model for the world.

Here is the checklist on American progress:

- Unemployment now stands at 8.1 million, an increase of 2.5 million since Bush came to power. Long-term unemployment has almost doubled as a result of 1.5 million jobs lost over the same period.
- There are now 32.9 million Americans living in poverty – an increase of 1.3 million. Median incomes have fallen for households in every income group, except for those earning over $150,000.
- Almost 800,000 Americans filed for bankruptcy in the first six months of this year – an all-time high. Home repossessions are also at a record level, with an average of 5 per cent of all home-buyers, 20 per cent higher than in 2000.
- The federal budget surplus was $86 billion two years ago. This year there will be a deficit of $314 billion, the third largest in history, except for two years in 1991–2 when Bush's father was president.
- There are 41 million Americans with no health insurance – an increase of 1.4 million. The cost of health insurance cover has risen by 12.7 per cent.
- Since Bush took over, there has been an overall increase in the crime rate of 2.2 per cent. The murder rate has increased by 3.1 per cent and the robbery rate by

3.9 per cent. The use of drugs has risen by 20 per cent, to the point where 6.1 million Americans are now in need of drug treatment.

- Air pollution is increasing and the number of times that poor air quality exceeded the health standard for ground-level ozone has almost doubled in just two years.

These figures[1] make terrifying reading because they reveal the sheer brutality of life for so many people who live in the richest nation the world has ever known. This is the nation that we are told is preparing to spend $200 billion dollars on a war that would inflict huge damage on one of the poorest nations of the Middle East – Iraq.

But they also tell us so much about the effect of following the policies so confidently recommended to us in Blackpool last week by the Prime Minister who is equally committed to that same deadly mix of policies: privatization, low taxes on the rich, means-testing of the poor and war with Iraq.

These figures should remind us that our own commitment to internationalism should include the closest cooperation with embattled American trade unionists as well as those in the Third World, because they too are struggling against the very same interests as those which dominate the IMF and the WTO, and are entrenched in Brussels, the Central Bank and New Labour.

Now that the media euphoria about New Labour's

---

[1] The figures I have quoted above come from the US Bureau of Labour statistics, the US Census Bureau, the American Bankruptcy Institute, the Mortgage Bankers of America, the Congressional Budget Office, the FBI, the Department of Health and Human Resources, the National Weather Service and other reliable sources.

'triumph at Blackpool' is being followed by the obituaries printed to commemorate the 'death of the Tories' as they meet in Bournemouth, we would do well to remember that the economic forces which dominate our politics, here and world-wide, are all the same. Until we move beyond the gossip that is peddled by the lobby correspondents who perpetually hover round the powerful and start analysing the root causes of the global tragedy that is slowly engulfing us we will make no progress at all.

11 October 2002

Ireland, Europe and the firefighters

After a second referendum, in which masses of money was poured in to secure a 'yes' vote, the Irish have been warmly congratulated, by the europhiles in London and Brussels, on their 'wisdom' in approving the Treaty of Nice which allows the EU to expand its membership and its control over us.

When we hear this result hailed as a triumph of European solidarity we ought to ask ourselves three questions. First, why was the first Irish referendum which opposed the treaty regarded as a 'mistake', and who decided to make the Irish vote again? Second, why did the Prime Minister ratify the Treaty of Nice on behalf of Britain without allowing the British people to vote on it in a referendum? Third, if there is a referendum on the euro in Britain, and we were to vote against it, would we be told if was a 'mistake' and compelled to have more and more referenda until we came up with a 'yes' vote?

It should now be clear to everyone that the whole

European integration strategy is completely fraudulent and we are expected to play the part of pawns in someone else's game. But this week we had another example of the true nature of the argument when the president of the European Commission – Signor Prodi – denounced, as 'stupid' the stability pact imposed under the Maastricht Treaty, also ratified by Britain by the last Conservative government without a referendum.

This stability pact, enforced by the European Central Bank in Frankfurt, prohibits the finance ministers in the EU, including Gordon Brown, our own Chancellor of the Exchequer, from borrowing or spending more than a certain percentage of our national income – which is a deflationary straitjacket.

During the boom years the German government was a firm supporter of these limits, but now, with high unemployment and lower economic growth, public expenditure in Germany is rising above these approved limits and so the rigid rules of the pact are being broken by Germany itself.

This is why Prodi – a passionate supporter of the euro – has been driven to denounce the way it is operating. In doing so he has annoyed the bankers because they see this as an attack on their powers, though neither Prodi nor the bankers have ever been elected by the people of Europe.

This is where the firefighters' pay claim comes in, because Gordon Brown may well be arguing that he cannot agree to meet their pay claim because it would lead to an increase in public expenditure above the limits of the stability pact. Here we have a practical example of how undemocratic it is for an elected government to be overridden by unelected bankers.

But that is not the end of the story, because the Prime Minister's determination to let private companies take over our public services, under the name of the private finance initiative, is also dictated by the straitjacket of the bankers. The pay claim and the pressure for privatization are closely connected, because the government's strategy is to authorize pay settlements only if those who get them accept this creeping privatization – all in the name of modernization.

This is also what the IMF is doing to the countries in the Third World who are being told that they can only get relief from the crippling burden of debt repayment if they agree to cuts in their own public services and accept privatization.

To sum it all up, what we are witnessing is the most determined effort being made here and world-wide to wind up the Welfare State and abandon our domestic democracy so that the bankers can run the world without any interference from those who have been elected to govern their own nations.

This is nothing less than the complete reversal of those democratic rights which we and people in many other countries have struggled to bring about, so the voters can gain some control over the rich and powerful.

This is the plain truth and we will make no progress until we recognize what is happening and resolve to do whatever is necessary to bring about a fundamental and irreversible shift in the balance of power in favour of the voters against the bankers. Having set out objectives we then have to plan to carry this policy through. It will be a massive task, but by no means an impossible one, providing we tackle it both at the national and the international level.

It is only when this is clearly understood by everyone that we can start making the move from the threat of globalization, which benefits the multinationals, to the reality of internationalism which embraces working people everywhere in policies of cooperation to improve our conditions.

Every generation has to learn its socialism by experience, and I suspect that that process of learning is going on quite fast – especially in the trade unions – which is why New Labour so detests the union link and would like to see it severed. That is why we must see to it that, on the contrary, it is strengthened and extended.

25 October 2002

Away with the Crown

The Prime Minister, like Paul Burrell, the loyal butler, has staunchly defended the Queen's decision to intervene to secure an immediate acquittal at the end of his long, expensive and unnecessary trial for allegedly stealing Princess Diana's property.

We are all expected to believe that the Queen had completely forgotten her three-hour talk with him; that she had agreed he was the best person to safeguard Diana's possessions; and that the injustice of his prosecution had never occurred to her until last week, even though it must have been discussed endlessly at the Palace for well over a year. The real reason for the Queen's intervention must have been that Mr Burrell was due to give evidence the following day and might, under cross-examination, have said something that threatened the monarchy and its popular appeal.

For the monarchy is the foundation on which the whole British power structure rests, and it is so important that the establishment might be ready to sacrifice King Charles III – as it did King Edward VIII, who was forced to abdicate in 1936 for fear that his marriage to Mrs Simpson might weaken the Crown and lead to a republican movement.

The monarchy also legitimizes a feudal class structure within which everyone is expected to know their place and keep it, bowing and scraping to those who are supposed to be superior in rank, like the Lords. In this way all those with privilege, wealth and power feel more secure from any challenges that might emerge from underneath, which is why radical leaders of the Labour movement are co-opted into the establishment by being offered peerages.

Nobody needs the monarchy more than the Prime Minister of the day, because the royal prerogatives are the source of most of the executive power that Downing Street uses, whereas a parliamentary majority only guarantees the passage of legislation, using the party whips who warn dissenting MPs that if they step out of line they might prejudice their chances of promotion or even lose their seats in a future election. These royal prerogatives allow the Prime Minister to go to war – as against Iraq – to sign treaties, to make laws in Brussels at the Council of Ministers which apply in Britain and to enjoy immense powers of patronage by stuffing the Lords with peers, and appointing archbishops, bishops, judges and the chairs of public authorities – all without any parliamentary authority.

Indeed, when the Prime Minister uses the royal prerogatives the House of Commons is powerless and MPs are not even permitted to debate any Bill which touches on the prerogatives without the express consent of the Queen herself. And to add insult to injury, every minister, MP, peer, judge, bishop, mayor and serving officer is required by law to swear a personal oath of allegiance to the Queen before taking office, even though, as an MP, they will have been elected.

The civil, military, police and security services, who are supposed to serve the government, do in fact regard themselves as servants of the Crown owing loyalty to the Queen and free to interpret that duty in the way that best serves the establishment (as when they keep socialists and trade unionists under surveillance). This is why even Labour ministers are never given the security files that are held on themselves.

The additional nonsense of the Burrell prosecution lay in the fact that all criminal cases are brought in the name of the Queen, and in his case it was the Queen who then had it dropped, while herself enjoying the privilege of personal immunity – as Queen – from being cross-examined as a witness on the statement she had made which led to his acquittal. Indeed, the very existence of a monarchy, at the head of what we call a democracy, is a complete absurdity and it depends upon the protection offered by the Prime Minister, which is always available because he needs its powers. In this way, Buckingham Palace and Downing Street work together, hand-in-glove, to keep the system going.

All those who argue for democracy are instantly accused of attacking the Queen personally, when actually she does not exercise these Crown powers herself, and has no effective control over their use. That is why republicans should never blame the Queen, as some do, for she didn't apply for the job. She was simply born of the right parents in the right bed at the right time, and she has a dull job which she has done for over 50 years.

What we should be demanding is much simpler and clearer:

- All royal prerogatives should be transferred from the Crown to the House of Commons so that the Prime Minister of the day would have to seek all his authority from elected MPs.
- The entire legal system should be disentangled from the nonsense that justice is dispensed in the name of the Queen and re-established independently as in all other civilized countries.
- The House of Lords should be replaced by an elected senate and the Church of England freed from state control.
- We should elect our own head of state, liberate the Windsor family to live their own lives, so we can get on with ours, and bring the Prime Minister under democratic control.

What a wonderful way to end the Jubilee year, and to know that it was 'the butler who did it'.

8 November 2002

War, fire-fighters and the future

After weeks of negotiation, a great deal of arm-twisting and some significant financial inducements, America bullied the UN Security Council into unanimously passing a

resolution demanding the return of the weapons inspectors to Iraq – which Saddam Hussein had agreed to some
weeks ago.

While the Prime Minister hailed this as an achievement
for British diplomacy claiming that he had persuaded
Bush to go to the UN rather than go it alone, the truth is
that Bush still regards the resolution that was passed as a
green light for him to attack Iraq. He was ready to wait
only because the huge military build-up had not been
completed and so the delay caused by the Security Council negotiations did not actually alter his timetable for the
war.

In any case, both Bush and Blair have made clear, time
and time again, that they believe no specific UN authority
for a war is needed. The war will be launched when the
necessary forces are in position.

For these reasons the interpretation of the latest resolution is of the greatest importance. The peace movement
has made it crystal clear that if and when the attack begins
we will not accept that this is a UN-authorized war that
we should support. For in truth such a bombardment and
invasion would be an act of aggression and a crime against
humanity, and every innocent Iraqi civilian who dies as
a result of British military action – and that could be the
fate of thousands – would have been killed on the personal decision of the Prime Minister, exercised without
even the authority of the House of Commons.

In effect, New Labour has gone along with a policy
which will amount to a decision to tear up the UN Charter and take us back to the law of the jungle, by siding with
Bush who has no intention of following the international
laws to which Britain is committed by solemn treaty.

And to make it all worse, the Prime Minister in his speech at the Lord Mayor's banquet on Monday warned of the danger that innocent people in Britain might be killed by a terrorist attack here, at the very moment when he is planning to do just that in Iraq, and at a time when he appeared at the Cenotaph on Sunday to commemorate the dead of two world wars in the usual Armistice day parade when we normally pray for peace.

The other issue at the top of the list this week is the thoroughly shabby way in which the fire-fighters have been treated – men and women who would be in the forefront of our defence in the event of a terrorist attack – just as they were in New York on September 11.

The government's behaviour can only be interpreted as meaning that the Prime Minister actually wants a strike to show that he is as tough as Mrs Thatcher was in dealing with the miners, back in the 1980s – an analysis that was confirmed when it was reported that Blair saw the fire-fighters as representing a return to 'Scargillism', a contemptuous reference to the NUM leader who courageously stood up for his members when they faced the destruction of their jobs, their industry and their communities.

Here are a group of very brave and highly skilled public servants who cannot afford to live where they work in London. The press has reported that the average house now costs £250,000, putting it way above what a public service worker can afford. (I believe that some who work in the capital actually commute from as far away as Wales and Nottingham.)

Moreover, following the Prime Minister's speech at the Blackpool conference last month about how he thought the state was too powerful and we needed more local discretion, it was the Treasury which vetoed the figure of a 15 per cent offer that had actually been offered by the local authorities to the fire-fighters.

The Bain Report, leaked to win public support, stuck with the 4 per cent, making, 'modernization' – a word that can be used to mean anything – part of the deal. (This is in marked contrast to the cut in MPs' hours that was also described as 'modernization'.)

And the argument that there are more applicants for vacancies in the fire service, which apparently justifies low wages, could also be used to cut the salaries of MPs and ministers, as even more people would like their jobs.

There is plenty of money for the projects which the Prime Minister favours, such as the Dome, the royal family and the impending war – but nothing on offer that in any way reflects the value of the fire-fighters' service to the community. Indeed, it is hard to escape the conclusion that everything the Labour movement and the Labour Party stand for is being deliberately ditched in pursuit of a permanent alliance with big business and Bush.

That is why we have to reclaim the Labour Party and work far more closely with all those deeply committed people who went to Florence for the European Social Forum, attended by around a million, which represents a movement here and world-wide for peace, democracy, internationalism and socialism. Its significance for the future could be as great as was the influence of the Tolpuddle Martyrs, the Chartists, Suffragettes and the early socialists here, a hundred and more years ago.

15 November 2002

Index

INDEX